"In this frenzied and fractured tir
seems to be the echo chamber of our days. Gary Agee's *That We May Be One* stands resolute in offering to the churches a distinctive voice and creative alternative to the usual zero-sum battles of our culture. To seek genuine unity, to discover what Paul intimated to the early communities, to experience fellowship with those we would discount, entails the risk of asking how it is with those beyond our comfort zone. By sharing his own humbling experience of seeking unity as well as wisely providing a rich array of resources, Agee invites us to discover that the desire to be one intimately ties the depths of divine life with the entangled reality of our life together on this planet."

— Arthur J. Dewey
professor of theology at Xavier University

"This book offers hope when many seeking unity may feel the pull of despair. On offer here is not a blissful, naive hope that is marked by optimistic delusion, but the hope that is found in attentive listening and acting to make biblical calls to unity come to pass. In this book, Gary Agee takes seriously the failures of the Christian church and the reality of societal and political polarization. Instead of succumbing to despair, he finds a thread of hope in biblical texts and glimpses of churches that show a trajectory of unity. Each chapter deals with Scripture, social realities, and practical challenges and opportunities for local congregations. He guides and inspires the reader to make the practice of unity a purposeful part of personal and congregational reflection and action."

— Nathan Willowby
dean of the School of Theology and
Christian Ministry at Anderson University

"Gary Agee's *That We May Be One* is a creative and courageous attempt to work at serious Christian unity. Agee is not naive in his desire for unity; as a Church of God pastor who earned his PhD at a Catholic university, Agee has broad first-hand experience of Christianity's fractured existence. With his lucid prose and his informative autobiographical anecdotes Agee makes a compelling argument for how we can move forward fruitfully towards a unified Body of Christ. One need not agree with Agee on all of his suggestions in order to benefit greatly from his important contribution. Anyone interested in Christian unity (and disunity) should prayerfully read this book."

— **Jeffrey L. Morrow**
professor of theology at Seton Hall University

"Dr. Gary Agee has provided both incredible research and personal story in this text. He offers the reader a new understanding about what unity is—and what it's not—and some ideas for making unity a reality. The close of each chapter provides discussion questions for groups and homework assignments to help each of us grow in Christ as Jesus prayed 'that they may be one.' Agee addresses the issues that divide us: race, gender, socioeconomics, LGBTQ+, nationality, religion, etc., in the hope that the reader will see how vast the inclusion/exclusion, us and them, is. It only takes one step for an individual to make unity possible—or to further alienate. Every person makes a difference. Thank you, Dr. Agee, for sharing your journey and your insight. I pray that we might be one."

— **MaryAnn Hawkins**
editor of *Called to Minister, Empowered to Serve*

That We May Be One

Practicing Unity in a Divided Church

Gary B. Agee

WILLIAM B. EERDMANS PUBLISHING CO. | LITURGICAL PRESS
Grand Rapids, Michigan | *Collegeville, Minnesota*

Wm. B. Eerdmans Publishing Co.
4035 Park East Court SE, Grand Rapids, Michigan 49546
www.eerdmans.com

Liturgical Press
2950 Saint John's Road
PO Box 7500
Collegeville, Minnesota 56321-7500

For rights, permissions, and sales,
contact Wm. B. Eerdmans Publishing Co.

28 27 26 25 24 23 22   1 2 3 4 5 6 7

ISBN 978-0-8028-8186-1

Library of Congress Cataloging-in-Publication Data

A catalog record for this book is available from the Library of Congress.

Biblical quotations are from the New International Version, unless otherwise
noted.

*For those who have yet to discover, just beyond the next hill,
further along, across the border—the face of God
in the "least of these"*

Contents

Preface

This book is born in hope. It is meant for individuals prepared to risk being carried along by the Spirit across divisive borders and boundaries, many of which are of our own making. It is meant to engage those who desire to see a united church living the unity for which Christ prayed in John 17 and are willing to model it for society. The audacity of a hope that imagines God's children thriving together, living in unity, does not escape me. Indeed, the din from the competing enclaves is deafening—sister pitted against sister, brother against brother. Wherever you stand, you can look in any direction and see that the church resembles broken asphalt on a neglected country road, with cracks stretching as far as the eye can see. In these polarized times we find ourselves separated by economic class, politics, ethnicity, theological loyalty, gender identity, race, sexual orientation, age grouping, a collection of moral questions, and other points of division. Sadly, we are all too ready to fortify these divides; we do this to our own hurt.

In the face of such disunion, at least two possibilities are within reach. One is to surrender to the darkness, to retreat from our diverse sisters and brothers, to close our ears, to continue shouting at one another over the walls erected out of fear and self-interest. A more compelling option is to make room to work on contentious differences and at the same time to learn more grace-filled ways to encounter one another. This more desirable alternative will require work, however. We must demonstrate the relational endurance to suspend judgment. It will be necessary to tamp down negative conditioning concerning the diversity we encounter. We also must open our ears to hear one another in the hope that respect, and even love, will spring forth. I contend that it is in this second option that together we will find a path to wholeness and become reconciled.

I despair to write of the practice of unity when factions in this country seem to be moving further apart. Indeed, there are partisans among us who thrive in such disunity. Division, after all, is a winning formula for some. And so the rhetoric of discord roars on as antagonists cheer with guttural approvals. It appears that if there were ever a season to give up on unity, it might well be this one. But despite the polarizing times in which we live, a central aspiration of the Christian faith is in fact the promotion of oneness. Moreover, as a disciple of a faith tradition (the Church of God Reformation movement) that has proudly trumpeted the cause of unity from its genesis, I seek to offer this book as a modest encouragement for the cause. I do so with trembling hands, knowing it is but a single bucket of water in the face of what feels to me like a wildfire—one that threatens the sacred sanctuary in which we all reside.

This book is penned primarily for people who live with privilege—folks like me, who might not think about border crossings every day, who expect things to work out, who have grown accustomed to getting to the front of the line and yet who are at least partially blind to the systems that have made such an advantage possible. You are my people; but like me you don't necessarily see that the way things have always been exacts an opportunity cost. There is a price for this inequity—one measured in disunity, layers of injustice, anguish, mistrust, animosity, and violence, now several generations deep. I extend this book, a gift of time and labor, in the hope that it will help those who desire to act for the sake of a redeemed future, one in which we meet our undisguised selves, make changes, and commit to moving, making room, and entering a new relational order. It is my hope that we can meet each other not as combatants but as allies—even sisters and brothers.

I do not offer this book as one whose vision has been fully restored. No way! Rather, I feel akin to the blind man who, when Jesus laid his hands on him, claimed only that he could see imperfectly. He saw people who looked like "trees walking around" (Mark 8:24). My hope for a full recovery lies in the hands of those who have been ignored or maligned, those who reside on the border with Jesus.

We begin this journey with the realization that God is present in our efforts to practice unity. We do not work alone. But neither do we sit around on our hands—blind, content, and comfortable—waiting for God to change our stony hearts. We partner together in this endeavor, with God, of course, but perhaps more important, we do so with our diverse sisters and brothers, no matter how the diversity they reflect is embodied.

My intent in this book is to offer a guide to what I believe could be the first few steps in a journey toward the practice of unity, an adventure we must not abandon before we reach the desired end. I realize that this map is incomplete and that it is but one of many plans that might yield similar positive outcomes. I celebrate these other offerings to the cause of the practice of unity. At the same time, I ask that grace be extended, especially from my sisters and brothers who live with injustice. As you well know, horizons of privilege promote and perpetuate blindness.

Finally, I suspect that asking tired souls worn out from fighting culture wars to take on a new campaign will draw a weary sigh. But unity—not fighting and gouging one another—is our purpose. We are willing to take it up because it is God's unfinished work. And though the endeavor seems to ask so much from us, it is nonetheless intimately attached to the Great Commission. We go to win the world, but we are well aware of the fact that we will never be able to reach the unredeemed in such a dysfunctional and divided state.

Division is our reality. To make a change we must begin somewhere. It seems reasonable to begin *by practicing the unity within reach*. Only after we take this first modest step are we in a position to muster the strength to trust God and our fellow diverse travelers in taking the next one. As we, in faith, open ourselves to God and to each other, we are drawn out beyond ourselves into the light—into a kingdom community unlike any we have ever known, one that is diverse and beautiful. In this new reality, we celebrate all God's little ones, from whom the light of God radiates.

Since taking up this book project, I have been encouraged by diverse scholars and church leaders to carry it through to completion even though I am white and serve in settings that for the most part embody societal privilege. Those who have been so supportive no doubt realize the benefits that can be gained by a serious study of the issues and systems that divide members of the body of Christ. At the same time, my access to an audience of similarly positioned individuals might also be put to use to encourage others who look like me to stretch and grow, to gain insight on how to live well, to be Christian in the best sense of that term, and to learn to thrive in the diversity within reach.

I suspect that part of my motivation for writing has to do with a lingering guilt for my complicity in the way things are. I ask myself: Am I willing to change, stretch, and grow—to love? Do I fully recognize the immeasurable worth in all of God's people? Have I really taken on the bigoted habits of heart and mind that tend to attach and then hold on stubbornly to us like cockleburs in the brush? Am I actively rewriting the narratives that have been used to shore up the broken status quo? Am

I willing to suffer isolation from my own people if I relate inconvenient truths we would rather not hear?

I acknowledge I have much to learn about the practice of unity, and I know enough to be suspicious when privileged individuals like me hold forth on such a subject. Carolyn B. Helsel, a white author who has written about racism, offers a compelling disclaimer: "I write this book out of my own anxiety, out of my own experiences of learning about racism and trying to find a way as a white person to join a larger movement of people working for racial justice. I'm not very good at it."[1] I might say the same about my own work on unity.

I find encouragement from Traci Blackmon, executive minister of justice and witness ministries for the United Church of Christ and senior pastor of Christ the King United Church of Christ in Florissant, Missouri. Speaking about the racial divide in this country, she asserts that white people indeed have a role to play in healing the breach. They can be allies. We are not to do the work of people of color, she contends, but to labor in solidarity alongside our sisters and brothers who chart the course toward justice. It is a work that necessitates honest and sincere effort. She writes:

> If you are serious about being an ally in antiracism work, there is another piece of work that has to be done. You have to be committed to reading; you have to be committed to educating yourself from a broad spectrum of resources; you have to be committed to watching not just the things that are made easy for you to see, but watching the things that might remain unseen, in interactions, communities, and environments. You have to be committed to listening for what is said and for what

---

1. Carolyn B. Helsel, *Anxious to Talk about It: Helping White Christians Talk Faithfully about Racism* (St. Louis: Chalice, 2017), 2.

is left unsaid. And for challenging those images and those instances that don't line up for what it means to live into a different way of being. . . . And allyship requires that you give yourself some space for grace.[2]

This book is limited in scope. Though I am convinced the practices set forth herein offer insight for the global church, prudence tells me that this work is best suited for readers in the United States. It is true that "people are people" around the world. Yet the divisions herein highlighted, as well as the initial steps toward unity prescribed, emerge from a particular context.

In the introduction I offer a disclaimer and an autobiographical sketch in "three acts." Using unity as a thematic guide, I tell a bit of my own story. Chapter 1 compares the pursuit of unity to a journey. Though the road traveled toward the fullest expression of oneness may be long, the adventure must begin with an initial step; we have good reason to get started. Chapter 2 offers working definitions of unity and the practice of unity. Chapter 3 sets forth what I label a "posture of unity," as I propose that deporting oneself in this way allows an individual to address diversity in whatever form it takes. Chapter 4 looks back at the transformation experienced by the disciples in the upper room and further proposes something similar for those seeking to engage the diversity blossoming all around us today. Chapter 5 looks at the Bible and unity, relying on what I label a "hermeneutic of inclusion" to draw out implications for the centrality of our relationships to others. Such a reading strategy also has implications for how we understand conversion and salvation. Chapter 6 examines distortions of the gospel currently promoted in certain segments of the church; some of these perverted gos-

2. Traci Blackmon, "On Being an Ally." Drawn from a series of adult education videos titled "White Privilege: Let's Talk," United Church of Christ, accessed September 13, 2019, https://vimeopro.com/progressrenew/white-privilege -lets-talk/video/172158957.

pels have been modified in order to stir up division. Chapter 7 offers some initial strategies to move folks from the "pew" to "practice." Finally, chapter 8 holds up three individual exemplars and one congregation for the benefit of those seeking to capture some sense of how the practice might be embodied.

At the end of each chapter I have included a section that I have labeled "Upper Room Exercises." These are to be used to carry the work of unity forward. An initial personal reflection allows space for an individual to "explore one's inner geography" a bit. This initial reflection is akin to what diversity training consultant Eric Ellis describes as "diversity conversations we have with ourselves."[3] A set of discussion questions follows. These conversation starters are meant to inspire group interaction around the topics of each chapter. In the "From Pew to Practice" exercise, I have included an idea that might otherwise be described as an action step. It affords the reader the chance to get started in the cause of unity.

3. Eric M. Ellis, *Diversity Conversations: Finding Common Ground*, 3rd ed. (Cincinnati: Integrity Development, 2019), 46–65.

Acknowledgments

This book would have been impossible without the help and encouragement of many. I offer thanks to the gracious individuals who gave of their time to discuss with me their insights regarding the practice of unity. Again and again I found encouragement in their inspiring efforts on behalf of oneness. A special thanks to James Ernest of Wm. B. Eerdmans Publishing Co. and Peter Dwyer of Liturgical Press whose shared commitment to the practice of unity breathed new life into this project. Most of all, I owe a debt of gratitude to Lori Lynn, my wife and best friend. Without her, unity would remain an incomprehensible mystery.

Introduction

An Autobiographical Introduction in Three Acts

Maybe we've been livin' with our eyes half open,
Maybe we're bent and broken, broken.
                              —*Switchfoot, "Meant to Live"*[1]

Allow me to begin with a disclaimer. I am a son of the church. She formed and shaped me. I sat under her teaching Sunday mornings, Sunday nights, and Thursday nights. In addition to these regular services, our family attended revival services, song services, and various other special church gatherings. Under a steeple, stretching upward toward the sky, I met many good people, including my wife and my closest friends.

In the last couple of years, however, a disillusionment has lodged within me, and I can't seem to shake it—even if I wanted to. But honestly, I'm not sure I want it gone. I'm not exactly sure when this happened or whether I am to blame for this sense of alienation. I feel more like the church left me. From where I stand, the faith of many of my religious sisters and brothers is increasingly unintelligible. My faith must appear to be of a

---

1. Switchfoot, "Meant to Live," *The Beautiful Letdown*, album released January 27, 2003. Columbia Sony/ BMG.

I

strange variety to them as well. I am sometimes confused by this fact; at other times, I am just angry.

In my public sermons I now speak more about structural evil, racism, gender inequality, social justice, and the need to practice unity. Yes, I still preach about salvation—after all, I hang mostly with evangelicals, but it is a salvation more thickly defined, one that includes more than a recitation of the sinner's prayer and a perfunctory "You're good now." Secretly, I fear that those with whom I worship have lost confidence in me.

I was converted and baptized into a divided church. I know this now. The sincere and pious members who gathered weekly in our sanctuary suffered, often unknowingly, from dislocation even as they harbored the very ideas and habits that perpetuated schisms. Though I did not realize this painful fact when, as a young child, I made a sincere decision for the faith, it would become more painfully clear throughout my years of development. When I knelt at the altar of prayer in our home church, I was twelve years old. On that evening, I not only received the blessing of salvation, but I also was unwittingly exposed to the germ of division. And I am even now feverish under its effects.

Act One

The year 1984 was a momentous one. At Christmas, only days before the New Year was to be celebrated, I had been given a small red journal by my younger brother. I suppose the prospect of recording my reflections each day appealed to my sense of self-importance. Anyway, I determined to take up the discipline of journaling. I didn't know what the year portended. As it turned out, that year would end in a painful broken engagement, and this difficult season of my life also blessed me with a good deal of unwelcome insight into just how hard it can be to practice unity within the Christian family.

As I prepared to make that first journal entry on January 1, I could look back over the previous months that had brought me to this new beginning. In May, just as I was preparing to graduate from high school, I had felt a distinct call to vocational ministry. I had enrolled part-time in a local university a few months earlier. I was in good financial shape as well, earning more money than I needed managing a local restaurant. With a sense of purpose, I began recording the events and musings that each new day presented.

Though I didn't realize it at the time, 1984 was a year that would mark my coming of age in another way. I was beginning to meet like-minded believers from other Christian groups. This led me to venture beyond my own family of faith—a modest-sized evangelical, nondenominational fellowship with a historical connection to the Church of God headquartered in Anderson, Indiana. This radical movement, birthed in the late nineteenth century, unabashedly proclaimed a message of holiness and unity. It later settled into a more ecumenical posture toward other traditions. Discipled within this group of dedicated believers, I was increasingly afforded the chance to practice oneness. I encountered Christians from other denominations, even as my university training introduced me to the world beyond my relatively insulated community.

As the buds sprouted on the trees and spring yielded to summer, I met and got to know a girl whom I will call PJ. Having recently received word from her doctors that her non-Hodgkin's lymphoma was in remission, PJ was just making her way back into the workplace. We both worked for the same fast-food franchise. Our relationship matured in conversations before and after work, in the break room, and between drive-through orders for cheeseburgers and shakes. These serious discussions went beyond music, cars, television, current events, and fads. In our minds we were destined to be saints, I guess; for this reason, we engaged in "God talk."

Theological and worship style differences separated us, but PJ and I were alike in many ways—sincere and committed to the Christian faith, at least as it was presented to us by those we loved and respected. We were both dedicated to living godly lives and to Christian ministry. Each of us was uniquely devoted to our respective church as well. We enthusiastically gave of our time and resources to the ministry. I was the guy who felt called to preach and toted around a fifteen-pound Bible. She was a guitar-playing miracle. From a distance, we were a match made in heaven.

PJ was much loved within the broad community of traditional Pentecostals residing in our part of the state. When she received the news that she had cancer, members related to this fellowship from all over came together in faith and took on this dreaded diagnosis. They prayed sincerely and passionately on her behalf as she grew dangerously thin and lost her hair. Defiantly, these people of faith claimed her healing—and in the end they prevailed. In the wake of this traumatic experience, PJ took up her tradition's strict proscriptions on dress: She wore no makeup, and she gave up her designer jeans, stylish dresses, skirts, and shorts for ankle-length alternatives.

PJ was Pentecostal—and I was, well, not that kind of Christian. This fact severely complicated our relationship. Somewhere along the way I had been led to view with suspicion people who practiced the gift of tongues and who worshipped in the emotionally demonstrative Pentecostal style. We even had a pejorative label ready for those who fit the description: They were, in our minds, "holy rollers."

Though looking back I can't recall the source of my suspicious thinking, I thought that Pentecostals were in general a misguided bunch. They obviously were not very thoughtful students of the Bible, particularly the sections having to do with the doctrine of the Holy Spirit and the practice of speaking in tongues. As for the dress codes, I saw no purpose for them. From where I stood, this legalistic practice did little to promote the kingdom of God; furthermore, it provided evidence that these wrongheaded believers were majoring in minors. I may not have been cognizant of it at the time, but we in our camp viewed Christians like PJ as "less than."

PJ's family and those with whom she worshipped felt pretty much the same way about me. As they saw it, I was a sincere seeker, but nonetheless incomplete, and at best a second-class Christian. This fact became painfully obvious to me when I spoke to her parents about our future together. They explained that she would not be happy in our church. These good-hearted people didn't have to tell me why. I knew. My church lacked the power and gifting of the Holy Spirit. This second-class status weighed heavily on me. How dare they! I tithed my income (really), I visited lonely and discouraged shut-ins, I was in church four times a week, I neither drank nor smoked, I read my Bible daily, and I led a small youth group. Despite all this I was viewed as worldly because I couldn't testify to a baptism of the Holy Spirit. In other words, I was viewed as "less than."

As I took up my pen to begin journaling, I found occasion to vent my frustration at such division. Our differences on the doctrine of the Holy Spirit and our disparate worship style preferences tore PJ and me apart. This divide was not a theoretical problem I had the leisure to curse from a distance. It was up close and personal, separating me from a woman for whom I cared deeply.

That little red journal details the painful daily saga that my relationship with PJ had become. I suppose that the keepers of our respective traditions had constructed well-intentioned warnings to keep folks like us from straying too far. To those with whom PJ worshipped, I was viewed as dangerous because I did not embrace the understanding of a baptism of the Holy Spirit evidenced by speaking in tongues. On the other hand, those in my camp viewed someone like PJ cautiously because she and her kind lacked the spiritual depth of Bible-centered Christians like us.

Unfortunately, the hostility that existed between our two camps was not uncommon in the hometown of my youth. In his popular book *Hillbilly Elegy*, author J. D. Vance describes his own dispiriting encounter with the religion he embraced as a young boy in Middletown, Ohio. He writes, "My new faith had put me on the lookout for heretics. Good friends who interpreted parts of the Bible differently were bad influences."

Vance further recalls how many of the sermons he heard as a young person were divisive in character and essentially critiques of the theological positions of other Christians. Not only were these same beliefs held up to scrutiny, but those who embraced them were also considered outside the Christian fold.[2]

Disunity and my inability to navigate differences within the Christian family occasioned within me a good deal of confusion and pain. This crisis came at a formative period in my faith development. Though I can't say I completely understood it at the time, it began to occur to me that something was lacking in the way we in the church negotiated diversity. At times it felt as though the body of Christ was divided against itself. Rival factions viewed each other as enemies, while well-worn Bible passages (often taken out of context) were used as ammunition. From the viewpoint of a young adult, these attacks detracted from our primary work.

Only a few days into 1984, I penned a poem expressing my dismay. This bit of adolescent verse I scratched down on an empty page in my large-print red-letter Bible.

> I've fought till I'm tired of fighting,
>   shield and spear in hand.
> No victory has been won,
>   for the enemy still does stand.

2. J. D. Vance, *Hillbilly Elegy: A Memoir of a Family and Culture in Crisis* (New York: HarperCollins, 2016), 96–97.

No assault has been made on his strongholds,
   no soul delivered from his snare,
But our charges have been against our fellows,
   not one of them did we spare.
We spend most of our time and our efforts
   trying to prove our fellows wrong,
While the enemy rests at ease;
   perhaps he sings this song:
"Will they ever get together? Will they ever see that
   the battle is not against one another, but against
   me, their enemy?"

As PJ and I prayed about our relationship, it seemed difficult to walk together in harmony. I had agreed to attend church with her part of the time, mostly for Saturday evening services. She came to my church occasionally as well. But this compromise didn't yield much fruit.

On one occasion we sat in the choir section, up front in her church's modest sanctuary. Our seat selection led to my further discomfort and alienation when the worship leader selected an old Pentecostal classic entitled "Pentecostal Blessing." Having had a different Christian upbringing, I frankly felt unable to join them in the lyrics, which testify to the authenticity of the Pentecostal experience. But those gathered in worship that night enthusiastically sang the polemical composition; it gives voice to the way many good Christians like PJ encounter the divine, but it felt to me like a wedge driving us apart:

It's real; it's real; praise God I know it's real;
This Pentecostal blessing, and I know, I know it's real!
It's real; it's real; praise God, I know it's real;
This Pentecostal blessing, and I know, I know it's real![3]

3. This song apparently circulates in several different versions. As far as I can

7

The song was likely written to answer the critics of this worship tradition, but in that moment, sitting in front of an enthusiastic crowd of believers, I didn't know how to respond. I felt like an outsider. One by one, worshippers stood to their feet to express their commitment to the Pentecostal experience as I sat stubbornly in my seat. When PJ stood, my heart sank.

We had both spent much of our lives in church, but despite the positive instruction and insight we gained, we inadvertently accumulated a set of denominational biases and prejudices that made it difficult to enjoy fellowship across denominational lines. In fact, it is this sort of denominational division that the Church of God reformation movement had historically opposed.

As I reflect on the entries in my journal from 1984, I realize that amid the pain that PJ and I endured together, we were afforded the opportunity to learn to practice unity. Having met her and her family, I was no longer able to view these Christians as less sincere or as unenlightened. I worshipped and served alongside them, and I witnessed their love for God. They were now my sisters and brothers in the fullest sense. It was because of our relationship that our cherished views about doctrine and worship were put to the test. I look back and see spurts of growth and moments of insight. For example, one evening after I challenged PJ about her dress code, I recorded a lament in which I confessed my own arrogance and insensitivity. My change of heart broke through the fog after PJ tearfully explained how difficult it was for her to dress in the holiness style. Up to that moment, I hadn't even considered her point of view.

After a couple of years PJ and I broke up. It wasn't just our theological differences dividing us, yet I feel that this relationship offered two young aspiring ministers the opportunity to

---

tell, it was written by a rugged coal miner named Nimrod Workman, although authorship appears disputed. *It's Real It's Real, I Know I Know It's Real, This Pentecostal Blessing*, YouTube, accessed November 23, 2019 at https://www.youtube.com/watch?v=odSHGoqKnus.

cross denominational borders for the sake of unity. Our respective faith communities were given the chance to stretch and grow as well. Though I did not fit the mold of the ideal Christian to those in her faith tradition, I was still a gift to them, as PJ was an unexpected blessing to those in my family of faith. There was no need for us to be anything less than the unique individuals God had made us to be. Pope Francis's words provide fitting insight in this regard:

> When the different theological, liturgical, spiritual and canonical differences which have developed in the Christian world are genuinely rooted in the apostolic tradition, they are a treasure and not a threat to the unity of the Church. To seek to do away with such diversity is to go against the Holy Spirit, who acts by enriching the community of believers with a variety of gifts.[4]

Act Two

As an undergraduate student at a local state university, I encountered the broad swath of diversity coloring God's world. To be frank, churches don't often exhibit a commitment to bringing together people with varied points of view and backgrounds. In rural churches across vast swatches of this country's heartland, the perspectives held by Christians of color, believers living in urban centers, affirming Christians, Latinx followers of Christ, and immigrant Christian communities are largely unknown. Sadly, this ignorance is often accompanied by a lack of desire to grow in understanding and insight. This lack of connectedness makes

---

4. Pope Francis, address to the Pontifical Council for Promoting Christian Unity, November 10, 2016, http://w2.vatican.va/content/francesco/en/speeches/2016/november/documents/papa-francesco_20161110_plenaria-unita-cristiani.html.

segments of the church susceptible to the nationalistic and xe-nophobic tendencies that often poison our congregations.

During my years at the university, I bumped into individuals from all over the world. I began to meet others whose perspectives were very different from mine, and my narrow perceptions were challenged. I grew as a result. I knew at the time something good was happening to me, and it did not feel as though this process of maturation was out of step with my faith commitment. This exposure to diversity, though it occurred outside the sanctuary of faith, helped me avoid the suffocating isolation we inhabit when we fail to venture outside our zones of familiarity and comfort.

Throughout my formal theological training, I have been blessed to cross boundaries and borders. Some of these cross-ings would have been unimaginable in earlier periods of his-tory. For example, my tradition experienced its genesis among nineteenth-century Protestant communities. Consequently, fellowship with Catholics was a bridge too far for these early pioneers. I didn't necessarily plan to attend graduate school outside my own faith tradition, but that's precisely where life circumstances led.

Upon completing my undergraduate studies, I landed a min-istry position I really wanted to keep. The best nearby option for a master's degree in theology was Xavier University, a Jesuit in-stitution in Cincinnati. I later completed a PhD in sacred theol-ogy at the University of Dayton, a Marianist institution. Though my choice to study among Catholic scholars wasn't understood by some in my tradition, it was nonetheless deeply enriching.

Pioneers in the Church of God, like many Protestants of the late nineteenth century, were strongly anti-Catholic. Old-timers in our tradition employed a label for people who followed the pope: They were "papists." Early Church of God leaders often took aim at the leader of the Roman Catholic Church, labeling him the antichrist. As devoted restorationists, they attempted to recover the purity and unity of the early church. To do so they had to return to a time before the papacy emerged and led the church into the "Dark Ages."[5]

Throughout my formative years, I grew up hearing how Catholics were insincere in their commitment to the faith, partying on Saturday and going to confession to clear it all up. This characterization was at times stoked by venerable church leaders for whom I had respect. I recall one of our regional gatherings, in which a seasoned church leader gave his talk on the Catholic Church. He obviously hadn't spent much time with Catholic believers. The institution he disparaged was nothing like the one I had known at Xavier and the University of Dayton. In fact, Catholic believers looked to me more like allies than sparring partners.

The growth I experienced during my years of graduate school, however, came at a cost. My ego took a hit when I first made my way to the floor that held the theology and religion books at Xavier's McDonald Memorial Library. I suppose seeing all those tomes and realizing how little I knew helped me to become a more proficient practitioner of unity. Though I had read the Bible, I hadn't even begun to take in the wisdom contained in this collection of writings. Indeed, there were many more lessons on the horizon.

Those within our movement generally hold a high view of Scripture. This set up one of my first academic cross-border challenges. I was privileged to study with a professor who was a member of the much-maligned Jesus Seminar, a group that challenged the long-held view that the historical Jesus actually said much of what is attributed to him in the New Testament. Certainly, our views differed when it came to whether Jesus actually taught what was printed in my red-letter Bible.

5. See, for example, Merle Strege, *I Saw the Church: The Life of the Church of God Told Theologically* (Anderson, IN: Warner Press, 2002), 104.

We both came, hermeneutically speaking, from very different places, and yet I learned so much from him, and after I completed a thesis defense under his direction he claimed that he had learned from me as well. Today I view him as a mentor, friend, colleague, and brother. He gave me my first teaching job, and he subsequently wrote recommendations on my behalf. The practice of unity across unlikely borders has its privileges, I suppose.

Act Three

My studies in history, Bible, and theology at the University of Dayton prepared me to examine race relations in my own faith community, the Church of God (Anderson). It was during these years of study that its schism along racial lines came into clearer focus for me. I read of principled women and men who chose to fight against racism and structural inequities. These same brave pioneers sometimes paid a high price for their devotion to unity. At other times leaders seemed to tailor their understanding of unity to fit the segregated Jim Crow system. These missteps, coupled with failures in our own era, have opened a deep wound that oozes mistrust, division, and pain—though we do not all seem willing to acknowledge it.

In the late nineteenth century, Church of God pioneers including Daniel S. Warner, Jane Williams, and Joseph and Allie Fisher "came out" of denominationalism and its divisions in order to promote the recovery of the purity and unity of the early church. For this reason, early pioneers routinely preached on the character of the church. These same standard-bearers believed it was impossible to live in unity within a denominational structure so divided along the lines of humanly devised creeds and constructions. The visible unity of the body of Christ was indeed important to these early believers, even if they didn't always recognize the potentially explosive social implications of the message they were preaching. African American church leaders like Jane Williams heard the message of unity differently than did their white counterparts. They understood that the promotion of biblical unity would necessarily address the obvious divisions created by the color line.[6] History shows that it took many years for white church leaders to catch up with God and these Christians of color. The history of the Church of God in southwest Ohio mirrors that of the larger movement, and this regional fellowship has been divided along racial lines from the earliest days. In this respect the Church of God is similar to many other denominational groups.

In the formative years of the life of the movement, women and men would give testimonials about their "coming out the confusion of Babel" into God's undivided church—the Church of God. They might on these occasions tell of going to a movement meeting where they would inevitably fall under the spell of a passion-filled Church of God evangelist. An exposition of the holy and undivided church that God willed would be set forth. This same compelling image would be placed alongside the humanly established sects and their "man-made" creeds. Somewhere in that tearful testimonial the old timers would declare "I saw the church" and then relate how they left their denominational affiliation to become a part of the Church of God movement.

I have my own experience with "seeing the church," and I share it because it relates to how I understand the practice of unity. My ecclesial breakthrough occurred unexpectedly on a Sunday afternoon in April 2002, in an African American con-

---

6. Rufus Burrow Jr., *Making Good the Claim: Holiness and Visible Unity in the Church of God Reformation Movement* (Eugene, OR: Wipf and Stock, 2016), xv.

gregation in my hometown of Middletown, Ohio. Up to that day, I had never been inside this particular church building, even though I grew up just over two miles away. I knew no one in the congregation except the pastor, who had often attended district-wide unity gatherings.

The meeting at the Eleventh Street Church of God was a fellowship gathering for the traditionally African American congregations of the Cincinnati district. Our suburban congregation had formally petitioned the black leaders of this consortium to ask for permission to become a member congregation.

In retrospect, the decision was naive on my part. I was a young pastor, and the congregation wasn't experienced in interracial community-building efforts. To be honest, much of the white cultural framework supporting the historical segregation of the movement was ensconced in our hearts and minds. Yet at the time of this petition it seemed like an appropriate first step, a way of reaching out to our sisters and brothers whom we had ignored for so long. It was a way of practicing the unity within reach.

In the spring of 2002, we were making a modest first step in our journey toward racial unity. The full expression of genuine unity—saturated as it is with respect and mutual love—would need to come later. It would have to wait on my people to come to terms with the prejudice hiding in the cracks and crevices of our hearts. We would have to unlearn centuries of negative stereotyping and ready ourselves to patiently hear stories of insult, injury, and injustice. We would have to lament, repent, and turn from our small-heartedness. Here, among the bruised and battered saints, we could finally hear what the prophets like Amos had to say to us. Indeed, on this particular Sunday we had only just begun.

After the greetings were spoken and the invocation offered, the worship leader selected a Church of God hymn cowritten decades earlier by Charles W. Naylor, a legendary leader among us. This same talented individual had been instrumental in promoting the charism of unity throughout the movement through his songs, hymns, and other writings. Though a great leader and an inspiration, he couldn't escape the racialization that tainted his era. For, like almost all of his contemporaries, he staunchly opposed the practice of interracial marriage:

> We teach that we should give no offense neither to the Jew nor Greek, neither to the church of God, as the Bible declares; or, in other words, we teach people to be subject to the social customs of the community wherein they reside. Most certainly we do not advocate the marriage of a white and a colored person, and I would not perform the marriage ceremony under such conditions even if the law did not forbid it. In all things we believe in both races keeping their proper places and relations.[7]

Just as important, this same author espoused a spiritualized definition of unity. This modified understanding made it possible to promote oneness without disrupting the racial divisions segregating society. Naylor writes:

> As for fellowship, that is not affected by race or color, as it is a thing of the Spirit of God, created in our hearts. "If we walk in the light . . . we have fellowship one with another" (1 John 1:7). This has no reference to any formal "fellowshipping" as they refer to in sectism. As to being separate in our worship, we do just as other people—observe the custom of the country.[8]

As a church historian, I thought of these sentiments as together we took up the hymn to sing on that Sunday afternoon. The enthusiastic response to this musical selection was unhin-

7. C. W. Naylor, column in the *Gospel Trumpet* (April 1, 1909), 9.
8. C. W. Naylor, column in the *Gospel Trumpet* (April 1, 1909), 9.

dered by the composer's past statements about race and racial intermarriage. The song's inspiring and idealistic rhetoric masked Naylor's suspect views on race. We raised the hymn as if we all believed it. In that emotional moment, the fourth stanza caught my attention: "Christians all should dwell together in the bonds of peace. All the clashing of opinions, all the strife should cease; Let division be forsaken, all the holy join in one, And the will of God in all be done."[9]

As if he were sensing my inner musing, the worship leader directed us back to that fourth stanza. We sang it again. In the wake of that second run-through, something happened. A saint of the Lord, moved by the song and carried along by the Spirit, stood up. She offered a spirited recitation of those same lyrics. "Christians all should dwell together in the bonds of peace. . . ."

She didn't merely repeat the words, however. She *chanted* them, her arms moving back and forth in a posture reminding me of a prize fighter. It was as if she was communicating that the sort of church called forth in the song would come to fruition only through determined effort and struggle—we would have to work for it. I *saw the church* that afternoon. I saw the church in her eyes. Oh, how I wanted to be part of the beautiful and diverse fellowship she was seeing—one in which the love of God flowed from person to person, a community where relationships would be made right. I wanted to be a part of this church, one that by its practice of unity would give credible witness to a divided world.

God's church is blessed with diversity of all types. Unity, by definition, assumes diversity. Stamping out diversity in the body of Christ constitutes a serious misstep. We may do it to make

9. Charles W. Naylor and Andrew L. Byers, "The Reformation Glory," *Hymnal of the Church of God* (Anderson, IN: Warner Press, 1971), 457–58.

ourselves feel more comfortable or out of some insecurity about the rightness of our own cause. But in the end we will find ourselves opposing God, who places each one in the body of Christ as he chooses (1 Corinthians 12:18). In the next chapter, we will look at the journey that is the pursuit of unity.

Upper Room Exercises

Reflection

Think about your own spiritual autobiography. How would you narrate your story if you were to use the practice of unity as a guiding motif? Scratch your thoughts onto a pad of paper. Over the course of a day or two, write down what comes to mind. Be honest: How have you benefited from the diversity of the body of Christ? Note also the ways you have been held back by its schisms.

Questions for Discussion

1. What sage advice would you give to a couple planning to enter an interfaith marriage?
2. Does your congregation hold a good record of welcoming people from different theological traditions? What about the "nones," those who don't belong to a faith? Is this practice of hospitality important to your congregation's leadership? Explain your answer.
3. Identify a particular religious group vilified by your tradition. Speculate as to why this might be.
4. Choose a religious group other than your own. List a couple of its key distinguishing characteristics or beliefs. What does this tradition have to offer the broader Christian community?

From Pew to Practice

Plan to make a cross-border visit to a worship service outside your denominational group. Prior to your visit, find out the core beliefs of that denomination or congregation. Try to keep a positive mindset by focusing on what you like or what you can learn from those folks. If you are really ambitious, make a list of similarities and differences between your theological tradition and theirs.

Chapter One

Getting Started

Unity can be accepted only by those who decide to set out on a journey toward a destiny that today may seem rather distant. However, those who follow this way are comforted by the continual experience of a communion joyfully perceived, even if not yet fully attained, every time that presumption is set aside and we all recognize ourselves as in need of God's love.

—Pope Francis[1]

I woke up one day and decided on a whim that I wanted to drive from my home in rural southwest Ohio to California. I had never visited the Golden State, so on this particular restless morning I must have felt deprived. Waiting on that distant coast was the Pacific Ocean, and I wanted to wet my feet in its cold blue waters. I wanted to see the Sierra Nevada, and those towering redwoods had always held a special place in my heart. So on this otherwise unremarkable morning I was ready—ready to head west.

With a brief gap in my schedule, I figured that a week ought to give me the time to get out there and back. By keeping to

1. Pope Francis, address to the Pontifical Council for Promoting Christian Unity, November 10, 2016, http://w2.vatican.va/content/francesco/en/speeches/2016/november/documents/papa-francesco_20161110_plenaria-unita-cristiani.html.

my half-baked plan, I would not have to disrupt my preaching schedule the following weekend. In hindsight, it would have made more sense to fly out, but at the time I figured I could do the trip more cheaply in my trusty Toyota, and by driving I would better appreciate the scenery along the way.

My college-aged son was skeptical. When I excitedly related my plan, he gave me a look and asked me how many cups of coffee I had consumed. I eventually talked two of my eight children into joining me on this whirlwind adventure. My skeptical son, however, was not among them.

Carried along by a spirit of expectation, the three of us made a start. We knew the trip wouldn't be easy. We would endure tedious miles of boredom, but in the moment, we didn't mind. The weather was good the first day and the driving easy. But on day two, an unscheduled snowstorm in Wyoming made traveling slow at first, then impossible. This unexpected delay cost us hours. Although I had checked the weather before we headed out, it didn't occur to me that a journey across the country in early winter might require more preparation. Once I saw signs advising the application of tire chains, I knew we were in for a ride!

Naively we pressed forward. The scenery along the way was incredible, to be sure: the Great Salt Lake inundated by a sea of white snow, the beauty of Yosemite National Park, and the majestic Pacific Ocean as it kisses the San Francisco Bay below Lands End Lookout. Wow! The adventure was indeed worth the effort, though I underestimated the rigors of the journey.

The journey toward unity can also seem arduous. At times it feels like driving with the expectation that just over the next hill you will catch a glimpse of your destination, only to find that what lies beyond is a valley with a thousand more hills to follow. Negotiating varying points of difference requires determination and patience.

Seasoned veterans who work in the borderlands of difference know that the pursuit of unity is hard work; it can sap one's energy.

I recently spoke with an older saint, one of the best among us. After broaching the subject of unity, she pessimistically responded, "We will never experience unity until we reach heaven." Another church leader working with a parachurch organization admitted she had stopped using unity as an aspirational aim, instead opting for less ambitious points of connection and cooperation.

In the quest for unity, there is, of course, the challenge of the many and varied ways disunity fractures the body of Christ. We are divided across a number of different fronts. To concentrate on only one of these difficult divides leaves the church subject to all its many other schisms. On the other hand, focusing more generally on all the ways in which we are divided certainly leads one to miss the complexity and intractableness of each divide.

When I first proposed this project, my goal was to move beyond the recognition that the church suffers from disunity, an observation that should be obvious to anyone. Instead, I planned to suggest practices that might motivate people to take action, to cross boundaries in order that we might begin to experience genuine unity with others—those near as well as those further away. It was admittedly a modest goal. And yet as the project moved forward and the complexities of these divisions came into clearer focus, even this modest aim seemed wildly ambitious. It felt like I had been relying on a faulty map reading. I wrongly believed we could cover the miles represented by each inch in a few relatively easy hours of driving. I was wrong. As it turns out, every inch on this map toward real unity equals a thousand arduous miles through incredibly difficult terrain.

The racial divide plaguing the church and society is perhaps the most intractable and disheartening. White Christians like me see the world quite differently than do people of color. After reading scholars and church leaders currently working to address white privilege, white superiority, and anti-black superiority, I wondered whether a book on unity was worth the effort. After all, many in the camp I inhabit simply wouldn't be able to digest much of this material without a serious investment in time and effort.

Far too many individuals with whom I travel talk more than listen. Our ranks are filled with self-proclaimed experts on gender, race, human sexuality, and a number of other divisive issues. This doesn't mean we have necessarily spent much effort studying such important matters. I suspect this tendency results from an undetected pride, which itself is a serious matter. More important, such pride masks a range of problems that we fail to see. For example, we often fail to consider the harmful ways in which privilege operates to the disadvantage of others. Systems long established in this country make it easier for some individuals to secure the resources needed to get ahead, while others are forced to the margins. Rationalizations supporting these systems and institutions have gained a level of undeserved acceptance, in part because of their constant repetition. These same justifications effectively push us further apart. In this climate of blindness and sometimes willful dishonesty, hierarchies forged far from the heart of God are permitted to tier the body of Christ. Generation after generation, these divisions are woven deeper into the fabric of our culture. Indeed, we have many miles of hard driving ahead if we want to experience the kind of unity and community God envisions for us.

Despite the difficulties, we must set forth on this journey. Border crossings are in our DNA. We need only look to the example of Abraham, who dreamed of a better country, one governed by God. This dream led him to gather his family and leave the comforts of his home to follow God's promptings. In a new land the patriarch built an altar to the God of border crossings; there in that strange and unfamiliar place the divine appeared to him (Genesis 12:1–7).

The fact that before his death Jesus prayed for unity might also inspire us to live and love into the oneness our Lord willed for the church. His petition still speaks to all who want to know the heart of the God Jesus sought to reveal. "My prayer is not for them alone. I pray also for those who will believe in me through their message, that all of them may be one, Father, just as you are in me and I in you. May they also be in us so that the world may believe that you have sent me. I have given them the glory that you gave me, that they may be one as we are one" (John 17:20–23).

In many circles, when we discuss prayer the formula is pretty well understood. People do the asking, and God is expected to carry out their expressed desires. Best-selling author Tommy Tenney says that in the case of Jesus's prayer for unity, however, the church bears the responsibility of answering it. He further contends, "Jesus' pleas for unity seem *to be the only unanswered prayers He ever prayed! His* prayer for unity—for oneness—remains unanswered to this day."[2]

We desire to be a people on the move, committed to reconciliation with God and willing to work toward the same with our diverse sisters and brothers—no matter the cost. Though this journey toward the fullest expression of unity might include twists and turns, disappointments and discouraging stretches, it is nonetheless worth the effort. Obsessing about the distance we must travel might also be unhelpful. For we find unity in the journey, along the route, in the difficult stretches as well as the pleasant downhill jaunts. Pope Francis recognizes this when he writes:

> From this point of view, unity, before being an objective, is a *journey,* with its road maps and rhythms, its slowdowns and accelerations, and even its standstills. As a journey, unity requires patient waiting, tenacity, effort and commitment; it does not annul conflicts and does not negate disagreements, but rather, at times it can expose us to the risk of new misunderstandings. Unity can be accepted only by those who decide to set

2. Tommy Tenney, *God's Dream Team: A Call to Unity* (Grand Rapids: Baker, 1999), 30.

out on a journey toward a destiny that today may seem rather distant. However, those who follow this way are comforted by the continual experience of a communion joyfully perceived, even if not yet fully attained, every time that presumption is set aside and we all recognize ourselves as in need of God's love. . . . Likewise, unity of love is already a reality when those whom God has chosen and called to form his people proclaim together the wonders that he has done for them, above all by offering a testimony of life full of charity to all (cf. 1 Pt 2:4–10). For this reason, I like to say that *unity* is *made by walking*, in order to recall that when we walk together, that is, when we meet as brothers, we pray together, we collaborate together in the proclamation of the Gospel, and in the service to the least, we are already united. All the theological and ecclesiological differences that still divide Christians will only be surmounted along this path, although today we do not know how and when [it will happen], but that it will happen according to what the Holy Spirit will suggest for the good of the Church."[3]

Thinking of unity as a journey is perhaps also important because it reminds us to avoid the pitfall of prematurely concluding that we've arrived. As sojourners along this path, we risk thinking unity is achieved any time we happen upon a comfortable stretch. It is important, therefore, to listen attentively to those who have suffered most the indignities and trauma of our disunity. We will know we have reached our destination when we *all* recognize—together—that we are finally home.

Enough, then, on how we might finish the journey. The pressing question is whether we make a good start. American society is dysfunctionally polarized. In our political spaces we snarl across fences and borders labeled "liberal" and "conservative." In

3.Pope Francis, address to the Pontifical Council for Promoting Christian Unity, November 10, 2016, http://w2.vatican.va/content/francesco/en/speeches /2016/november/documents/papa-francesco_20161110_plenaria-unita-cristiani .html.

the church, of course, we have our own sets of schisms regarding sexuality, biblical interpretation, church governance, and so on. Huddled in fortified camps, we ascribe the worst motives to the groups we oppose, blaming them for this plight while shielding those in our own group from any responsibility for the hostile state of affairs. Some have given up and grown accustomed to the dark. (Some, alas, even relish it.) But for individuals who realize that something is amiss, for those willing to walk toward the light they see in the eyes of those on the other side, can we find a place to make a start? I offer the following ancient Chinese proverb from the *Tao Te Ching*: "A journey of a thousand miles begins with a single step" (chapter 64).

Going to the Gate to Make a Start

Once I preached a sermon on the parable of the rich man and Lazarus (Luke 16:19–31). In this biblical account the rich man lives a life of careless affluence.[4] The troubling narrative further illustrates the greed that had created so much indifference on the part of the rich man toward poor Lazarus. As I worked on the message, however, the details of the story struck me in a new way. I detected, for example, a disturbing "fixedness" in the account. The rich man seems stuck; he can't learn; he is immobile. He can't meander down to the gate and experience some sort of relational breakthrough. In short, the account leaves no room for the rich man to repent by getting to know and love Lazarus.

Jesus's story sketches the lives of two men who lived differently even though they resided in close proximity. The rich man did well for himself; he had the finest clothes and all he wanted to eat. And he erected a barrier to separate himself from the poor and destitute in the community—from people like Lazarus.

---

4. Luke Timothy Johnson, *Sacra Pagina: The Gospel of Luke* (Collegeville, MN: Liturgical Press, 1991), 3:254.

Walled up on his estate, he lived in privilege. He wasn't at all concerned about the plight of the poor beggar at his gate.

Lazarus on the other hand lived a difficult existence. He likely was crippled since he was placed by others at the rich man's gate. He constantly battled hunger. Lying in tantalizing proximity to plenty, Lazarus slowly withered away in want. Under the watchful eye of heaven, he grew ever thinner. The hungry dogs that prowled the neighborhood licked the sores marking his body. His was a miserable existence.

The way the parable is written leaves the reader hungering for more details. How did the rich man know Lazarus? What was the nature of their relationship? Did the rich man's servants speak ill of Lazarus? Did they think he suffered as a result of some flaw in his character? Was the rich man Lazarus's distant relative? Was the wealthy estate owner callous or simply neglectful?

Upon the death of both men, a great reversal occurred. Lazarus now enjoyed all he wanted, including the comfort of Abraham's protection, while the rich man found only torment. In his desperate state, the rich man longed for the poor beggar to cross the divide separating them so that Lazarus could bring a refreshing drop of water to ease his pain. Prior to his death, Lazarus must have also desired this same sort of visit from the rich man. But no one had come down from the house to offer him food or comfort.

Another detail that caught my eye is the fixed nature of the divide separating the two men at death. The opportunity to share resources had passed. The image of this permanent chasm nonetheless offers hope to the living and breathing: the divides that torment us, that keep us from growing together, are yet penetrable. There is still time to cross over. One can still make the journey out to the gate and beyond in order to minister to and be enriched by those whom we encounter on the other side.

Sharing this message poses challenges in a congregation that has more in common with the rich man than with Lazarus.

I asked myself, "Where is the hope for me and my people in this account?" With an eye toward our community's need to repent, I explained to the congregation that it might be good to renarrate the story in a way that would illumine a path of repentance for the rich man. It seemed to me this road to reconciliation would necessarily begin with his coming to terms with the deprivation and suffering of the beggar at his gate. Once this sensitivity was stirred up, then the rich man might have been motivated to make some real changes.

The renarration I shared with my congregation looked something like this:

As the rich man sat at his table, stuffed from eating a tasty afternoon meal, he noticed that, though the guests had eaten and the servants had taken their portion, still there was plenty left over. Not only was there bread, but there were even some precious scraps of meat. What would he do with it? He hated to see it go to waste. Some of the surplus he could store, but part of it would not keep more than a day or so.

Precisely at that moment, Lazarus came to his mind. Though the rich man had seen the beggar from a safe distance, he did not know him. True, the rich man's servants had more than once complained about Lazarus being placed at the gate. The wealthy man had even agreed. But the leftovers would either go to the stray dogs or to Lazarus. In the end, the rich man sent a servant to carry the scraps to Lazarus.

When the servant arrived at the gate and offered the food to poor Lazarus, he wept. The beggar lifted one hand to God. His prayers were answered! He blessed the rich man as well as the servant. It was a heartfelt thanks. And when the servant returned to his master's house, he related the poor man's genuine gratefulness.

That evening the rich man could not sleep. He thought about Lazarus and the servant's account of the beggar's gratefulness. In the wee hours of the morning, as he mulled over what the servant had related, he decided that he would visit the gate himself the next day. Upon completing his meal the next evening, he packed some of the leftovers from the table. Then, to his servant's astonishment, he gathered the food and headed to the gate where Lazarus had been laid. He greeted the beggar. Lazarus turned toward his wealthy visitor and motioned him to come near. In a soft voice the old beggar, with tears streaming down his cheeks, blessed the rich man.

After that first encounter, the rich man made his way to the gate every evening. There was something warm and genuine about the beggar. He seemed to have a way about him that the rich man could not quite explain. When the two men were together, they talked—about life, about God, and about family. Without knowing why, the rich man looked forward to these conversations. And with each visit the beggar could expect plenty to eat. The meals continued even when the wealthy estate owner was away traveling for business. For he left explicit instructions for the members of his household to make sure Lazarus was fed.

On one of the feast days, the rich man asked his servants to go to Lazarus and ask if he might care to join him and his guests for the celebration. Though he had to be carried, the beggar came with joy. When he arrived, the rich man gave him an expensive cloak dyed in purple. The beggar was soon reclining in the place of honor next to the rich man. Though the other guests could not understand the reason for the gesture, none dared to speak their mind. The music, dancing, and mirth were unlike anything Lazarus had ever seen. As much as anything, the rich man enjoyed Lazarus's excitement over the party. From that day forward, neither fence nor wall could interrupt the budding friendship between these two unlikely acquaintances.

One day after the two had eaten together, the rich man became serious in tone. "Is there anything you need?" He asked his newfound friend. "Yes," Lazarus replied. "I have many friends who are too feeble to work; some are sick; some are crippled; others have no home; and they are all hungry. A number of them have been abandoned by their families. If I had your great wealth, I would build them a shelter and make sure every day that they were all fed."

The rich man responded to the request enthusiastically. "Of course, you are right. If this is what you think needs to be done, then we will build a grand shelter together. Since I met you, Lazarus, I feel as though I have been able to draw insight like cold water from a deep well. You have showed me what living is really all about." The rich man knelt down to where Lazarus was seated, and the two men embraced. This time the tears were in both sets of eyes.

Work on the shelter began right away. Though there were many buildings within the walled compound of the rich man, the two were determined the shelter would be the most ornate. But before the building could be completed, the poor beggar died. The rich man, pained at the loss of his newfound friend and partner, determined to give him a proper burial. As was the custom in the land, the wealthy estate owner brought in mourners to weep for the passing of Lazarus.

More determined now than ever to complete the project, the rich man gave the order to expedite the work. Soon it housed the community's most needy daughters and sons. Servants who once had run to meet every whim of the rich man now looked after the destitute souls gathered in the shelter. As the rich man passed through the building each day, he would often speak of his friend Lazarus. And until the day of the rich man's death, not a single meal was served in his own house until provision was made for those gathered at the shelter. Moreover, he had made plans to supply the shelter beyond his own death.

One evening, after a brief illness, the rich man also died. But he did so with few regrets. He had made restitution to those he had wronged, and so he was buried in peace. There was a marked difference in the rich man's passing and that of his wealthy peers. For the friend of Lazarus had many mourners who were poor, blind, and sickly. These were the rich man's new friends; and they wept tears of genuine sorrow.

In death the wealthy man opened his eyes. He seemed to be at home. And coming toward him was a horde of beggars. Lazarus, decked in a purple cloak, led the happy and raucous band.

This blessed homecoming had begun with a single step, a decision to bridge a divide. Indeed, it began with a trip to the gate.

Welcoming All Who Gather at the Gate

The need to cross boundaries and practice unity is not merely theoretical. The demographics in this country reveal a changing landscape. By 2045 the United States will become a "white minority" country, meaning that as a total percentage of the population nonwhites and those who identify as multiracial will outnumber whites. White Americans are projected to make up 49.7 percent of the population, Hispanics 24.6 percent, African Americans 13.1 percent, Asian Americans 7.9 percent, and those identifying as multiracial 3.8 percent.[5] Moreover, the majority of Americans believe that being black or Hispanic hurts their chances of getting ahead economically.[6]

5. William H. Frey, "The US Will Become 'Minority White' in 2045, Census Projects," Brookings Institution, September 10, 2018, https://www.brookings .edu/blog/the-avenue/2018/03/14/the-us-will-become-minority-white-in-2045 -census-projects/.

6. Anthony Cilluffo and D'Vera Cohn, "6 Demographic Trends Shaping the U.S. and the World in 2019," Pew Research Center, April 11, 2019, https:// www.pewresearch.org/fact-tank/2019/04/11/6-demographic-trends-shaping-the -u-s-and-the-world-in-2019/.

Income inequality also threatens the cohesiveness of the country. In 1971 roughly 61 percent of Americans were considered middle-class. By 2016 that number had dropped to about 52 percent. In addition, income inequality continues to increase the gap between America's wealthiest citizens and those most at risk. Among Asian Americans this gap nearly doubled between 1970 and 2016.[7]

The American family is changing as well. In 1968 only 7 percent of parents who were living with a child were unmarried. By 2017 that percentage increased to 25 percent. Many of these same parents are now responsible for caring for an adult. American women are also choosing to work at a career and so are having fewer children than in previous generations.[8]

Changes in the church mirror demographic shifts in the larger population. Juan Martinez, a professor at Fuller Theological Seminary, points out that traditionally white congregations are shrinking even as more diverse groups continue to swell. Some religious denominations and groupings seem to model this racial and ethnic diversity better than others. According to Martinez, those embodying the most racial and ethnic diversity include the Seventh Day Adventists, Roman Catholics, Assemblies of God, Church of God (headquartered in Cleveland, Tennessee), and the Churches of Christ. These developments demonstrate the need to work and minister in a setting different from that of previous generations. Practicing unity well will be critical for ministry success in the future. In the next chapter, we will take a closer look at the kind of unity that will help to develop this diversity.[9]

---

7. Cilluffo and Cohn, "6 Demographic Trends."

8. Cilluffo and Cohn, "6 Demographic Trends."

9. Juan Martinez, "Imagining Browner Churches: Being Faithful Christians in a Changing Society," *Vision: A Journal for Church and Society* 18 (2017): 33–40, https://press.palni.org/ojs/index.php/vision/article/view/57/27.

Upper Room Exercises

Reflection

Which groups in your community are unrepresented in your church? Gauge your own willingness to share your fellowship with a wider population of potential attendees.

Questions for Discussion

1. Recall a memorable vacation or excursion. Compare the positive and negative aspects of this trip with your own journey toward the experience of unity. Share your thoughts with the group.
2. With an eye toward unity and inclusion, review the story of the rich man and Lazarus (Luke 16:19–31). What insights come to mind?
3. What do you make of the rich man's posture toward the beggar at his gate? Which of the two men possessed more ability to bridge that gap? Explain your response.
4. Identify the "Lazaruses" lying at your gate. What obstacles (internal or external) keep you and those within your fellowship group from "going to the gate"?

From Pew to Practice

Review the census data for your community. Educate yourself regarding your community's diversity. Note the possibilities for practicing unity beyond your demographic. Get up and "go to the gate."

Speaking of Unity

Unity is where heaven and earth meet. It springs forth at the intersection of loving God with all one's heart, mind, soul, and strength, and loving neighbor as oneself (Mark 12:30–31). Unity is born of paradox, holding diversity and oneness together in perfect balance. It is fueled by our highest ideals, and yet if it is to be judged as authentic it must be concretely incarnate in our real-world and sometimes contentious relationships.

Unity Defined

How do we define unity? In much of the literature on this important subject the definition is assumed. Oneness implies harmony and agreement. For the believer this coming together is joined to the conviction that God initiates unity and that this oneness is brought to fruition in the work of Christ. Indeed, unity results from our reconciliation with the triune God. God initiates it, but people have the opportunity to embrace and grow into it—or, if we so choose, to resist it.

One might say that Christ is the "hearth" around which we Christians gather. Outside the fold of the faithful, believers see a world where relationships are characterized by greed, selfishness, and injustice. Inside the beloved community, however, members are meant to experience the warmth generated by living in harmony with one another in God. But this Christocentric unity fueled by God's love need not be hoarded. The unity of the faithful is a womb from which many offspring are born, each in turn producing its own measure of reconciliation. Believers in Christ must learn to press into this more expansive understanding of unity.

Unity in Christ is not as easy as it might first appear. Complicating this discussion are the many different understandings of Jesus. Believers often thwart the experience of unity in part because of the promotion of distorted images of Christ. Curtiss DeYoung cautions us in this regard: "Our modern understandings of Jesus are often a far cry from the real Jesus of Nazareth who walked the earth during the first century. We have misinterpreted, reinterpreted, misused, and remade Jesus to serve our own purposes."[1]

Unity is not the sole possession of any one Christian sect or group. It is simply too large and expansive, as it finds its genesis in God's love for the entire world. Where God's love is shared, unity in some measure and form is manifested. It is not to be delimited by a particular tradition's creeds or narrowly defined "truth."

With a more broadly conceived understanding of unity, the faithful are free to establish different "hearths" around which people can gather and enjoy one another's company. From these various points of agreement and fellowship, we can roll up our sleeves to work together for justice, equality, and the betterment of the world. It is also necessary to recognize that these points of connection find their source in God. Given that God loves the world, it is important to see individuals from other religious traditions—or no tradition at all—as partners. The practice of unity can't help but carry believers beyond the borders of the Christian faith, but it always does so in a posture of love and service.

---

1. Curtiss Paul DeYoung, *Reconciliation: Our Greatest Challenge—Our Only Hope* (Valley Forge, PA: Judson, 1997), 37.

Where unity is encouraged, a spirit of camaraderie and connectedness binds together individuals on opposite sides of contentious moral issues as well as those of different races, class groups, ethnicities, gender communities, political affiliations, age groups, and sexual orientations. It is by definition more than mere tolerance; it is fueled by love for neighbor. Saturated with generosity and the desire for the good of the other, unity implies a willingness to celebrate difference—or at least to bracket the point of disagreement in order to maintain relationship. Though sometimes separation is necessary for the integrity of a cause, the commitment to unity puts it off until absolutely necessary. It seeks rather to walk in fellowship with the diverse other. Unity requires watchfulness on the part of its keepers. It is provisional and in constant need of maintenance. It calls all who commit to follow it to stretch (sooner or later) to the breaking point.

The pursuit of unity is not tangential to the practice of the faith—it is our work; it is our witness. For many who call themselves Christian, unity finds its source in the doctrine of the Trinity. In this respect unity might be imagined as the spilling over of the communion of God into the relationships of ordinary people. As the Roman Catholic catechism explains: "The Church is one because of her source."[2] The Second Vatican Council's decree on ecumenism, *Unitatis Redintegratio*, puts it this way: "[Unity] is a mystery that finds its highest exemplar and source in the unity of the Persons of the Trinity: the Father and the Son in the Holy Spirit, one God."[3]

Unity is where heaven and earth meet. It springs forth at the intersection of loving God with all one's heart, mind, soul, and strength and loving neighbors as oneself (Mark 12:30–31). Unity

2. "The Church Is One," *Catechism of the Catholic Church*, 813, http://www .vatican.va/archive/ccc_css/archive/catechism/p123a9p3.htm.

3. Second Vatican Council, *Unitatis Redintegratio*, Decree on Ecumenism, http://www.vatican.va/archive/hist_councils/ii_vatican_council/documents/vat -ii_decree_19641121_unitatis-redintegratio_en.html.

is born of paradox, holding diversity and oneness together in perfect balance. It is fueled by our highest ideals, and yet if it is to be judged as authentic, it must be concretely incarnate in our real-world and sometimes contentious relationships. It is akin to authentic faith in that it must "work" in this world or be viewed as "dead" (James 2:17).

Though unity might be conceived as an end goal, it also is partially present in every reconciliatory act that leads us toward the establishment of a just community. The practice of unity can be exercised at any point along the journey toward oneness. At times practicing unity might be modeled by going on retreat in order to meditate on a problematic relationship. It might mean finding a counselor in order to negotiate differences with a spouse, coworker, or alienated family member. Someone who reads to understand the challenges faced by women in the work-place is engaged in the practice of unity.

PRODIGAL UNITY

In the parable of the lost son (Luke 15:11–32), it is possible to discern the practice of unity in several of the generous father's acts of reconciliation. Each of his gestures was meant to create oneness in what seems to be a fractured family unit. The story ends with the forgiving father pleading with a second alienated son to attend his wayward brother's homecoming party.

Yet a closer look at this story reveals that the practice of unity occurs throughout. For example, after the younger son unabash-edly insults his father, the older man lets him leave with his inheritance. One can empathize with the father who no doubt felt disrespected and abused by his misguided child. But still the father let him go. More tellingly, the father retains the hope that his self-willed offspring might someday have a change of heart and return home. Throughout the ordeal the father refuses to succumb to bitterness. All such actions on the part of this gracious father model the practice of unity.

When the younger and disgraced son returns penniless and hungry, the father abandons any sense of retribution, embracing him wholeheartedly. This display of the practice of unity is not conditioned by the son's sincerity, for the story leaves one with the impression that the younger son is motivated to return home simply because of his hunger and deprivation.

The practice of unity is evidenced throughout the remainder of the parable. The spontaneous party thrown for the younger son emphasizes the spirit of welcome toward one who has strayed far from home. It is also possible to see the practice of unity in the father's dealings with the elder son. For example, he expresses his love for his older charge even as he attempts to persuade him of the importance of receiving his younger sibling back into the family. The story ends with the conflict unresolved. And yet the father demonstrates the posture of unity throughout.

Unity can be incarnate in a handshake, a card, a kiss of charity, an invitation to a meal, or an offer of a listening ear. It might be expressed in a march, a protest, or in a political campaign to move society closer to equality. Unity can be recognized in the reconciled face of a sister who has been welcomed back into the family. Oneness is intimately related to what evangelicals call revival and renewal. In its fullest expression, it requires that society's unjust systems be set right—those that privilege the few at the expense of the vulnerable.

In the pursuit of unity, one must look out for those who peddle cheap and inauthentic counterfeits. Addressing the role of women and men in Eastern orthodoxy, Rachel Cosca observes that the promotion of a circumscribed kind of unity can be used to maintain the status quo or to silence women on the margins.[4] Cheap or false unity, though it may be passed off as

---

4. Rachel Cosca, "Just Unity: Toward a True Community of Women and Men in the Church," *Ecumenical Review* 66, no. 1 (March 2014): 39.

authentic, does little to address the inequities that privilege one group above another. Cosca writes: "Cheap unity is unity without justice, unity without repentance, unity that displaces the majority of the human and Christian family from its visioning. We cannot pretend that healing theological divisions within the church can be separated from the need to heal divisions within the human family."[5]

In this book, I address unity broadly across various of points of division. Why not just stick to a single cause of disunity? I follow this strategy in part because of my training as a diversity consultant. Often when I am called in to work with an organization, management is interested in addressing a wider scope of potential points of division. This approach makes sense because, for example, working with mostly white audiences, it is sometimes easier to illumine ways in which privilege tracks with race and gender while also discussing other diversities, including education level, income status, able-bodiedness, and sexual orientation.

Another reason to take up a more broadly focused approach to the discussion of unity is because forms of discrimination working against unity often overlap. This insight comes by way of the theory of intersectionality, which gets at how prejudice operates in society. Various kinds of bigotry are often "intertwined." They form an alliance of resistance against unity and reconciliation. For example, those negatively impacted because of race often find themselves disadvantaged because of their class status as well. Similarly, women of color find that both race and gender must be accounted for in any discussion of privilege.

I suspect another reason for addressing disunity across a number of fronts is that many feel comfortable tackling divisions in selected areas but are less inclined to do so along other points of difference. Some, for example, are willing to work to-

5. Cosca, "Just Unity," 48.

ward racial reconciliation but are not interested in practicing unity with members of the LGBTQ community. Practitioners of oneness should proceed cautiously here. Unity restrained in any area stunts our ability to cross boundaries well. To circumscribe and restrict unity is to ruin it. It is necessary to bear in mind that heartlessness always breeds division, no matter what form that heartlessness takes, or what justification we craft to support it.

Let us not kid ourselves; doing unity is hard and exhausting work. The practice of unity takes perseverance and patience. I once interviewed a denominational leader who spoke frankly about the difficulties he had experienced along this front. He labeled it "spiritual warfare." Indeed, when we take on the work of unity it feels at times as though the devil has been loosed.

Years ago I worked alongside a pastor who displayed a commitment to unity. With regard to promoting oneness, he was a standard-bearer. I loved him for his consistent witness in this regard. He purposely crossed ethnic and racial barriers, always exuding a spirit of love and service in his effort to promote oneness. On one occasion, however, he came to me visibly moved. I don't recall the venue, but I won't forget the scene. Tears were streaming down his face. I had never seen him like this previously. Frankly, I had seldom seen any minister display the kind of transparency and brokenness he communicated to me on that day. Clearly he was facing a crisis that had put him back on his heels. He explained that he had been recently harried and harassed with racist thoughts. It was obvious he was deeply troubled as a result.

How could I have helped but to consider my own brokenness in this moment? In terms of practicing unity, my friend was far ahead of most folks I knew at that time. As I look back at this encounter now, I wonder how individuals are able to hold prejudicial views but at the same time remain unbothered by them. I have to believe that if we were in step with the Spirit and honest with ourselves and others, we would see the need to make our way to the mourner's bench. The process of honest introspection of the sort displayed by my friend is a necessary step on the road to oneness.

As has been said before, the practice of unity is difficult. But we should press forward nonetheless. John Perkins gives us reason to hope in our seemingly impossible task:

> We serve a mountain-moving God! It will take nothing less than His mountain-moving power to bring us together as one. We must ask Him, believing that He can accomplish this great task. I've heard it said that we should regularly pray prayers that are so big that only God could accomplish them. I believe that. And we shouldn't be afraid to ask God to do the impossible, because we know His record. He's not afraid of the impossible, from opening the Red Sea to raising Lazarus from the dead. All impossible deeds. But He did it. And He can make us one together. . . . He can do it![6]

When God works to bring relational healing, it can begin in the most unlikely of ways. You simply don't know when or how it might occur, because in these instances it doesn't appear to be guided by human efforts. The following story might illustrate this point.

One Sunday a set of unexpected circumstances made it possible for our rural congregation in Ohio to host a Rwandan refugee I will call "Della." She had come to the United States for a brief stint to promote her book. Her story was harrowing. As I recall, she had lost her husband in the Rwandan genocide, and she had witnessed the murder of members of her own family. She gave birth in the middle of the ordeal. That she and her children escaped death was a miracle.

---

6. John M. Perkins, *One Blood: Parting Words to the Church on Race and Love* (Chicago: Moody, 2018), 151.

On this particular Sunday, a middle-aged man I will call "David" attended. On the surface he shared little in common with Della. She was a woman from Africa, decked in a beautifully colored traditional dress. He was dressed in a pair of jeans and T-shirt—the short sleeves of which revealed a collage of tattoos on both arms. David is a military veteran and patriotic. He listens to talk radio, and his politics are conservative. He loves cars, bikes, trucks, and four-wheelers. He is creative and superb at woodworking. If he was going to be stereotyped, he would pass for "biker" or possibility a "good ole boy."

Della, on the other hand, left Rwanda and moved to Germany. As a result of the trauma she suffered, she went through a long period of recovery. Subsequently Della began writing and working to support a nonprofit benefiting both victims and perpetrators of the violent conflict. On this particular Sunday, she shared her story in the best English she could muster. She spoke for about half an hour. It wasn't particularly easy to understand her. She also spoke rather quickly. Members of the congregation had to listen carefully in order to follow her horrifying account. But for David who was seated in the back of the church, the message came through loudly and clearly.

Following the service I sent Della and her ministry partner to the back of the congregation so members of church could greet them as they exited. Following the benediction I glanced back toward the couple to make sure they were OK. There in the center aisle, as big as you please, David had swallowed Della up in a full embrace. I have seen lots of hugs in my time, but this one was different. I could feel something. It looked so strange. David hugged her like he had found his long-lost sister. They talked for a brief minute, and he embraced her again.

A couple of weeks later David and I had the chance to speak after church. He related how God had ministered to him through Della's testimony. The sincerity in his expression made that point clear to me. Rwanda is several thousand miles and an ocean away from the rural community where David and I live. But God's kingdom knows no borders or boundaries. To put it succinctly, God used Della to communicate his love and presence to David. Such are the blessings of unity.

Given that both the church and society are confronted with many forms of disunity, taking on a posture of unity in order to negotiate any one of a number of these challenging divides seems to be prudent. In the next chapter, we will take a closer look at what it means to take up this posture of unity.

Upper Room Exercises

Reflection

Think of the differences that lead to disunity both inside and outside the church. Which do you have the most trouble negotiating? Why is that?

Questions for Discussion

1. How has your understanding of unity been stretched as a result of reading this chapter? Which characteristic of unity stands out most? Explain.
2. In the story of the prodigal son (Luke 15:11–32), the elder brother appears to be bitter toward his father and younger brother. Had he maintained a commitment to practice unity, how might this story have been told differently?
3. List four community goals in which you might find "common cause" with individuals who embrace no particular faith tradition. How might you begin to work together to reach these mutually important aims?
4. How might an individual or group avoid settling for a false or counterfeit form of unity?

From Pew to Practice

Choose the area of difference that gives you the most trouble. Commit to reading about it from a perspective different from the one you now hold. Following this exercise, list five key learning points. Commit to incorporating these new insights in your daily interactions with others.

Chapter Three

Taking on a Posture of Unity

I find it particularly troubling when people claim an intimate knowledge of the whisperings of the heavenly realm and yet appear to be so completely deaf to the pain of marginalized communities in our midst. I have become convinced that only when we train our ears to hear those whom society considers "the least of these" will we genuinely pick up the frequency of heaven.

One who desires to work for unity must adopt sensitivities and skill sets that allow them to bridge differences across a number of fronts. It is therefore important that one take on a posture of unity—that is, one must take up the habits and sensitivities of one who negotiates diversity well. Like an athlete who competes in the decathlon, mastering skills that are transferrable from one sporting event to another, one who takes on a posture of unity must adapt to any difference that may arise.

Drawing on the work of Howard Thurman and James E. Massey, Curtiss DeYoung embraces something like the posture of unity I imagine. He describes the ministry of reconciliation as something like a lifestyle or discipline. He writes, "We must embrace reconciliation as a spiritual discipline—as a godly habit. . . . We must integrate reconciliation into our living in such a way that it becomes as normal and life giving as breathing. Our ability to serve as instruments of God's reconciliation requires that we pray that God's thoughts inform our own thought process every day."[1]

Similarly, one who desires to practice unity must embody a range of sensitivities, virtues, and habits of heart and mind. This discipline or way of living in the world makes it possible to welcome diverse individuals into one's company with grace and wisdom. It is not, however, a habit that one puts on for special occasions and then sets aside for the rest of the time. Rather, negotiating difference in whatever form that it takes must become integral to one's life.

In adopting a posture of unity, one need only embody the sensitivities, virtues, and habits that should otherwise be present in the life of any follower of Jesus. When we act in humility, when we are transparent or patient, when we commit to listening to one another, we exhibit the traits of people who have taken on the posture of unity. We also thereby model what it means to be a believer. In speaking of the lifestyle of people who are reconcilers, Curtiss DeYoung writes, "Only as we exhibit more and more of the likeness of Jesus Christ can we fully embrace the ministry of reconciliation."[2]

HUMILITY AND THE POSTURE OF UNITY

Humility before God and before others is an essential aspect of a posture of unity. Samuel G. Hines reminds us that the "first manifestation of unity is humility."[3] Each individual has a place in God's kingdom. We all have gifts, insights, sensitivities, and

1. Samuel George Hines and Curtiss Paul DeYoung, *Beyond Rhetoric: Reconciliation as a Way of Life* (Valley Forge, PA: Judson Press, 2000), 7.

2. Hines and DeYoung, *Beyond Rhetoric*, 7.

3. Hines and DeYoung, *Beyond Rhetoric*, 52.

abilities. There is no hierarchy in the body of Christ. Rather, we come together as sisters and brothers, none more important than another to God or the work of the kingdom. Though this affirmation is easy enough for the average Jesus follower to acknowledge, it isn't always lived out.

A posture of unity requires that we know our place. We are not God. Our judgments of others are always incomplete and in some measure distorted. Knowing this should encourage us to listen and move with more care in handling the differences we encounter. We are at our best when we hear one another, when we pull up alongside those we meet as different or misguided. When we meet others, we should never stray far from the fact that we ourselves are yet maturing and developing.

Humility is easier to maintain when we realize that we have horizons that block our view; we simply cannot see all that God sees. Limited in our capacities, we stand before the ocean of God's richness with an eight-ounce paper cup. There is no way that we can contain all there is to be received from above. God's richness is immeasurable, and this bounty is shared with his offspring the world over—daughters and sons all. It is helpful to remember that our siblings are as graced as we are; perhaps they see as much as we do, maybe even more. When we come to understand that others might well be just as dedicated as we are to the cause of right, we are in a better position to make room for them, even if these same individuals don't hold all our cherished convictions.

Humility is also characterized by a willingness to admit one's own faults. We must cultivate the sensitivity and skills necessary to examine the geography of our inner lives. In short, we must come to terms with how we have been socialized, malformed, bent, and broken along life's journey. We must repent for our individual missteps and see our culpability in the operation of the systems and institutions that privilege some over others. Finally, humility demonstrates a readiness to do the hard work to grow and change, a hunger to know and mature, a passion to pursue the work of God in this world, and a commitment to maintain unity.

Listening

Conditioned by a proper sense of who we are, we are positioned to take on a second characteristic of a posture of unity, the ability to listen—to both God and others. Anyone trained in the art of communication realizes that listening is a skill difficult to master. Listening requires us to address both the filters that distort our interactions and the barriers that block them altogether. These filters and barriers come in various forms. The most sinister, however, appear to be those we harbor within us. These strong biases and prejudices effectively eclipse our field of vision. We must acknowledge these impediments.

Being open to the voice of God is paramount in the life of the follower of Jesus. Jim Daly reminds us of the time commitment required of one who wants to hear from God. He writes:

> We may feel as if God is saying something to us after a period of time, putting a message or impression on our hearts. But it's important to sit quietly with that and continue to listen. Often our richest experiences with the Lord come after a sacrifice of *time*. We do well to sit at the Master's feet, as Mary of Bethany did, listening intently without feeling rushed by the things that need doing. What could be more important than hearing and then responding to his words to us?[4]

---

4. Jim Daly, "The Importance of Listening in Today's Evangelicalism," in *Still Evangelical? Insiders Reconsider Political, Social, and Theological Meaning*, ed. Mark Labberton (Downers Grove, IL: InterVarsity Press, 2018), 181.

Some well-meaning folks seem to hear from God on a regular basis. At times, however, I have puzzled over what they claim to hear, as it is hard to reconcile what God is telling them with reasonable efforts to build a just and equitable community of faith. I find it particularly troubling when people claim an intimate knowledge of the whisperings of the heavenly realm and yet appear to be so completely deaf to the pain of marginalized communities in our midst. I have become convinced that only when we train our ears to hear those whom society considers "the least of these" are we genuinely picking up the frequency of heaven.

The willingness to listen to others is an absolutely essential aspect of a posture of unity. As practitioners of oneness, we don't merely listen in order to formulate good counterpoints. Nor do we listen in order to find points of comparison with our partners in conversation. We don't even listen to empathize. Rather, as Traci Blackmon points out in speaking of listening in the context of interracial conversations, we listen to understand.[5] Conversations with those who view the world differently offer both parties the opportunity to grow. Again, Jim Daly writes, "Being a good listener is a basic act of service and humility. It honors the dignity of the individual. People aren't offended or put off when someone is attentive to what they have to say. We gain and grow not [by] displaying what we know but by listening well to what others have to say and considering what they can teach us."[6]

According to diversity consultant Eric Ellis, we can enter four types of conversations: open, closed, learning, or challenging. In an open conversation it is possible to take on a different point of view. In a closed conversation, however, it is difficult

5. Traci Blackmon, *On Being an Ally*. One in a series of adult education videos titled "White Privilege: Let's Talk," United Church of Christ, accessed September 13, 2019, at https://vimeopro.com/progressrenew/white-privilege-lets-talk/video/172158957.
6. Daly, "The Importance of Listening," 182.

to even hear what the other is saying, much less make use of the insight being communicated. A conversation in a learning mode allows one to increase knowledge of a subject. Finally, in challenging conversations, one actively resists the other's point of view. Each of these approaches has its place, Ellis acknowledges, but for our purposes a posture of unity requires healthy engagement across lines of difference. Employing Ellis's classification of these interactions, it appears that open, learning, and even challenging conversations offer the most promise.[7]

In closed conversations, however, the inability to listen to other opinions runs counter to the cause of unity. Studies show that it is rare for individuals to seek out information that might broaden their views. Psychologist Dolores Albarracín, who directed such a study, writes: "If you are really committed to your own attitude—for example, if you are a very committed Democrat—you are more likely to seek congenial information, that is, information that corresponds with your views. . . . If the issues concern moral values or politics, about 70 percent of the time you will choose congenial information, versus about 60 percent of the time if the issues are not related to values."[8]

Conversations that attempt to negotiate differences can be emotionally charged, as anyone who has tangled with an ideologue of any stripe knows. What is important in these conversations is that each person be heard and that the interchange be characterized by mutual respect.

7. Eric M. Ellis, *Diversity Conversations: Finding Common Ground*, 3rd ed. (Cincinnati: Integrity Development, 2019), 98–101.

8. Dolores Albarracín, quoted in "Those Unsure of Own Ideas More Resistant to Views of Others," Eurekalert, accessed July 14, 2021, at https://www .eurekalert.org/pub_releases/2009-07/uoia-pss062509.php. See also "Feeling Validated Versus Being Correct: A Meta-Analysis of Selective Exposure to Information," *Psychological Bulletin* 135, no. 4 (2009), https://www.ncbi.nlm.nih.gov /pubmed/19586162.

INTROSPECTION AND THE PROCESS OF SOCIALIZATION

Important to sustaining a posture of unity is the ability to examine one's own thoughts and feelings. I am not proposing a formal process of introspection under the guidance of a professional facilitator. I am instead encouraging the development of a more relaxed habit of self-reflection, one which allows an individual to examine the influences behind conscious thoughts and deeds. It could be said of many of us that the geography we know least about is that which lies within us. In this regard we don't seem to be a very curious people. There is so much about us hiding out below our responses, decisions, words, and actions. We don't regularly turn our critical eyes inward. As a result, the contours of our inner life—the mountains, valleys, oceans, and caves carved out by those who have influenced us, including our families, our peers, the media, our church tradition, or our experiences, to name but a few—remain largely uncharted. And yet it is from this inner region that the weather systems that shape our life decisions and opinions, our thoughts and feelings, are generated. We must pay attention to the net result of this socialization process. We have been shaped (and certainly *misshaped*) by these forces. Mustering our powers of critical reflection for this challenging and eye-opening exercise is good practice for one who seeks to take on a posture of unity. Moreover, this kind of work is productive in that it grows our self-awareness.

Socialization can be described as the preparation and training we receive to be a part of a group or society. It can be formal or informal. This formation begins at birth and continues throughout our lives. The lens through which we see and experience the world is shaped significantly throughout this lifelong learning process by those with whom we travel. Individuals and other cultural influencers all have a hand in this development. The fruit of this socialization can either prove helpful to building genuine community, or it can lead to conflict and disunity.

We are often affected by our socialization more than we realize. For example, if someone was raised in a home where slurs were used to describe members of the LGBTQ community, it colors the way that person views those individuals. Or if someone was raised in a family where interracial dating was frowned on, the damage has likely been done without even being registered. Such malformation must be constantly scrutinized and managed.

Growing up in a relatively homogenous and insulated community may make it more difficult to negotiate differences. Lack of awareness about the forces shaping one's perspective obstructs the possibility of understanding another's point of reference. When working toward unity, therefore, it is helpful to remember that others may have been conditioned in very different circumstances, and they will see the world quite differently.

The sum total of our malformation makes it more difficult for us to engage others in a healthy and respectful manner. Much of this training, therefore, must be "unlearned" over time. The process of critically examining one's own faulty formation is necessary if one is committed to a posture of unity. In this process of unlearning one might, for example, commit to tracking down biased bits of information that historically served to inform one's perspective. A person who has taken up the task of unlearning might ask the following: "Why do I think the way I do about this diverse group of people or that issue?" "Is this information consistent with how things really are?" "Where did I pick up this attitude or thought?" "Is my thinking in line with what it means to be a disciple of Christ?" As layer upon layer of conditioning is pulled back in this quest of unlearning, one will need to decide whether particular ways of thinking ought to be retained. Moreover, a process of unlearning will require that the individual seek out information from beyond his or her regular relational network.[9]

9. Rhetorically speaking, unlearning is a helpful idea. I suspect unlearning

Self-Awareness

A commitment to introspection will result in a measurable growth in self-awareness. Yet some of the ways in which we are complicit in working against unity are harder for us to see than we care to acknowledge. Scripture speaks of two individuals who went to the temple to pray (Luke 18:9–14). One was a despised tax gatherer and one a religious leader. Whatever else one makes of this biblical account, one thing is obvious: It is the tax collector who possesses a more accurate sense of his own failures.

On the other hand, the pious Pharisee seems clueless as to his own waywardness. Instead, he proclaims his righteousness over against that of the tax collector. Regarding matters of unity, we often fail to recognize the biases attending our interactions with diverse others. We can claim, for example, that we have absolutely no prejudice toward a person of color, while at the same time employing language and tropes that betray that claim. The Pharisee was blind to his own faults and failures, but God was privy to them. Similarly, it is likely others see our own faults, even if we can't.

In 1955 psychologists Joseph Luft and Harrington Ingham created Johari's Window, a technique used to enhance self-awareness and improve interpersonal relationships. What stands out in this method is the acknowledgment of unknown areas of the self as well as parts of our lives we prefer to conceal. We tend to be blind to some sectors of our lives, while we guard against showing hidden portions to others. It is in the push and pull of relationships, however, that these concealed areas come to light. Growth comes when we can reduce both the "unknown self" and the "hidden self." Insight from the use of Johari's Window provides a way of discussing these unmapped and hidden areas.

Eric Ellis points out that the self-perception of individuals who are self-aware generally lines up with the way others see them.

---

is much more difficult than I suggest here. Maybe the best most of us can do is to manage the faulty thinking that serves to distort our respective worldviews.

These enlightened individuals are also able to admit to themselves and others their biases. Finally, they are willing to receive feedback from those with whom they interact; sometimes they even seek it out.[10] Ellis continues, "Those individuals who have an accurate view of themselves are better equipped to monitor their thoughts and behaviors in order to make appropriate adjustments to create healthier discussions with others who are different. The lack of self-awareness ranks as one of the most frequent characteristics of a person ineffective in relating with others."[11]

Ellis further offers a number of strategies that encourage growth in self-awareness. These include focused self-analysis, encouraged by what the author labels "intellectual curiosity"; developing a process for receiving continuous feedback through the use of formal testing instruments including the DISC Personality Assessment Test, the Myers–Briggs Type Indicator, and the Harvard Implicit Association Test (IAT). Along with these approaches, one might spend time studying one's social environment or engage a personal feedback coach.[12]

TRANSPARENCY

The willingness to be transparent is an important element in a posture of unity. If we are ever to get anywhere in our dealings with diverse others, we must be able to acknowledge our own limitations while making plenty of room for others to be imperfect. After all, the practice of unity is a trial-and-error proposition.

One of the biggest diversity problems in our society, Ellis argues, is the unwillingness of people to acknowledge or be transparent about their own biases. Often this reticence results from the fear of stigma.[13] He writes, "There is a significant ben-

---

10. Ellis, *Diversity Conversations*, 59.
11. Ellis, *Diversity Conversations*, 54.
12. Ellis, *Diversity Conversations*, 59–65.
13. Ellis, *Diversity Conversations*, 92.

efit gained when people move from a posture of denial, fear, and complete ignorance of their biases to clarity, ownership, and accountability. As more people begin to admit their human frailty, there is less time and energy wasted on meaningless debates."[14]

Some biases are easier to admit than others. Ellis found that many in his workshops were willing to admit to "surface-level biases" that do little to move the conversation forward, while "deep-level" biases are more difficult to own up to.[15]

I recall once picking up one of my sons after a basketball game. He had just received his driver's permit, so I planned for him to drive us home. As he jumped into the passenger seat, another car recklessly flew past us. Thinking this incident had set up a perfect teaching moment, I said, "Did you see that? That was probably a kid driving." My son paused a second, then delivered the perfect deadpan response: "Mr. Diversity." With this short, poignant quip, he forced me to admit the foolishness of my assumption. Had I not driven long enough to know that reckless driving is no respecter of age?

Perhaps transparency is easier when we realize that we all have issues on which we must work. When a relative of mine was still a teenager, a skunk had gotten under his house. He wasn't foolhardy enough to go after it, so he instead simply went to bed, thinking it would leave on its own. At some point that evening, however, the skunk sprayed the house. Though he had not been sprayed directly, the odor could still be detected by his friends at school the next day, much to his embarrassment.

Similarly, our perceptions have been impacted by decades of problematic conditioning regarding people who inhabit the margins of society. I would contend that we, too, have been

14. Ellis, *Diversity Conversations*, 95.
15. Ellis, *Diversity Conversations*, 94–95.

tainted by our proximity to the indirect conditioning in society, just as my young family member was affected by the skunk's indirect attack. By recognizing this point, perhaps we may be better positioned to make a recovery. A first step, then, is to welcome transparency and to acknowledge the odor of complicity emanating from us.

A Holy Curiosity

One useful ingredient for taking on a posture of unity is curiosity. We often gather in separate enclaves together with those with whom we share common traits, and we find it awkward to engage those with whom we differ. In such isolated enclaves, it is easy to hold uninformed and problematic views of others.

If we maintain what I call a "holy curiosity," however, we may mitigate our isolationist tendencies. On the last day of a diversity training class, for instance, our group had thoroughly covered the curriculum. The readings had been completed, the videos viewed, and all the exercises collected. Our group had discussed how we had been impacted by our upbringing, and we had examined how mental models form and function. We had also introduced the concept of critical thinking as it relates to issues of diversity. In this final session, we were enjoying snacks as we wrapped up our time together.

Before the class dispersed, however, one of the students—without giving the matter much thought—made an overtly racist comment. I was taken aback, as were the other students, who looked to me for an appropriate rebuttal. So I responded with a question, one I have returned to repeatedly in similar situations: "Are you curious?" In other words: Have you already made up your mind, or are you open to receiving new light on the subject at hand?

To practice unity we must be fired by a holy curiosity to know more, to see more, to understand more. We must never be like those whom Jesus condemned for having "calloused hearts," and eyes and ears that they willingly closed (Matthew 13:15).

Relational Endurance

Finally, one who takes on a posture of unity must demonstrate some relational fortitude. Establishing meaningful connections across boundaries and cultural borders is not for the faint of heart. The opportunity for friction or even outright offense is constant. Unless there is a strong commitment to walk with those on the opposite side of an issue, it is often easier just to part ways. But we serve a God who does not so easily give up on broken relationships. All through the Bible God pursues a wayward people. We too ought to carry a persevering commitment to reconciliation.

In the next chapter, we will examine the "re-formation" experienced by the disciples as they fellowshipped and prayed together in the upper room. It may take a similar season of transformation if the disciples of our generation ever hope to minister in a way that promotes oneness.

Upper Room Exercises

Reflection

A number of "habits and sensitivities" mark someone committed to a posture of unity. Rate yourself on these traits. Reflect on which one you might want to improve. For example, how well do you listen to others?

Questions for Discussion

1.   Besides Jesus, which biblical character best demonstrates a posture of unity?
2.   How does your church, religious group, or denomination promote the kind of "habits and sensitivities" that mark someone with a posture of unity?
3.   Think of the last time someone really took the time to listen to you on a deep level. How did this exchange make you feel?
4.   Which of your close acquaintances best models the posture of unity?

From Pew to Practice

Choose one habit or sensitivity from those presented in this chapter. Commit to an hour reading more about its importance in relation to the maintenance of healthy relationships. Share what you have learned with a spouse, friend, child, or coworker.

Chapter Four

The Upper Room Experience

The church today at times feels like it is situated somewhere between the ascension and Pentecost. Perhaps what we need is to return to the upper room to relearn how to relate across the divides that separate sister from brother. God will meet us there, yet we have a part to play as well.

The social conditions that foster the fullest expression of unity are not easily established. For people to genuinely come together in their diversity, major matters must be set right. Unity doesn't flower in communities fraught with distrust, mutual fear, and repressed animosities. Nor can it reach its fullest measure in a world obsessed with wealth, privilege, and power. If we believe that unity is God's desire for the church, then this same God must necessarily be at work in us to create an atmosphere where unity can flourish. We must only get with the program.

A number of problematic factors complicate our coming together in oneness. First, meaningful exchange and connection across areas of significant difference require that individuals be motivated by a genuine desire to engage the other. For too many church folk, however, this doesn't seem to be the case. We have grown comfortable in our divided state. What happens elsewhere is not our problem. Second, those who seek to engage differences must address the conditioning that serves to distort the way we think about a group on the other side of an issue or boundary. If we hold flawed views about ourselves and others, it seems that partnering with God in order to do diversity well is hampered from the start. Underneath our interactions with others is an operative system of values. We live in a world that gives place to the wealthy, the powerful, the talented, the beautiful, and the well positioned. Far too often, we in the church are guilty of adopting a similar system of tiering. For real unity to flourish, this must be unlearned. Finally, unity invites us to see the world through the eyes of others. It is difficult to imagine unity flowering among us when there is so little overlap in how we experience what lies before us.

Having over the past two decades researched the racialization of American society, the abiding schism along the lines of race increases my pessimism about unity's future among church folk. The invisibility of white privilege enjoyed by those in the dominant group, coupled with the rationalizations circulated to support the way things are, makes the prospect of coming together across this chasm difficult to imagine. Too often, well-meaning white Christians cannot understand what underlies the frustration of people of color. For example, I recently spoke to an individual deeply committed to caring for the less fortunate in our community. She had been working to improve the lives of others for much of her Christian life. Her faith in God and her compassion for those in need is evident to all. Yet still, she found inexplicable some of the criticisms raised by an African American she encountered in her ministry. How can unity really occur if we can't get close to getting on the same page?

I am at least partially aware of the risk of injecting race into a project about the practice of unity. I'm not sure this book would enjoy any credibility without such a discussion, however. I suppose, too, that bringing up racial privilege makes some feel I am placing too much blame on people who look like me, but I don't see it that way. My goal is unity. For us to get there we must lose our blindness as to how the world works, and we must avoid rationalizing the inequities around us. From our perch of privilege, hemmed in by such distorted rationalizations, we have a long way to go to get to the common table where unity is practiced.

When Brenda Salter McNeil draws attention to the way these distorted accounts of racial difference affect white folk, one can hear unsettling echoes of affirmation from a long line of prophetic black leaders. As she points out, white individuals seem disturbingly unaware of the impact these distorted narrations have on their identity.[1]

Even those interested in the work of reconciliation have trouble recognizing the way in which their particular culture has distorted their thinking. McNeil writes, "I often see this as a college professor working with young white students who are eager to engage in the work of reconciliation but who seldom realize the degree to which they are also in bondage to the system of race. I am convinced that until they go through a Holy Spirit-led process of awakening, they will remain in a state of blindness."[2] It is naive to think one can practice unity in the fullest sense unless one realizes the extent to which our own malformation puts distance between us.

When we begin to give an accurate accounting of the inequity privileging the dominant racial group in this country, it will be equally important to stop accusing people of color of bringing up the issue illegitimately. Many individuals who look like me do not want to discuss the myriad of ways race privilege is manifested. Why not? In her compelling treatment of what

1. Daniel Hill, *White Awake: An Honest Look at What It Means to Be White* (Downers Grove, IL: InterVarsity Press, 2017), 1–2.
2. Quoted in Hill, *White Awake*, 1–2.

she labels "white fragility," Robin DiAngelo clarifies part of the reason for this pushback. She writes of white individuals:

> Socialized into a deeply internalized sense of superiority that we either are unaware of or can never admit to ourselves, we become highly fragile in conversations about race. We consider a challenge to our racial worldviews as a challenge to our very identities as good, moral people. Thus, we perceive any attempt to connect us to the system of racism as an unsettling and unfair moral offense. The smallest amount of racial stress is intolerable—the mere suggestion that being white has meaning often triggers a range of defensive responses. These include emotions such as anger, fear, and guilt and behaviors such as argumentation, silence, and withdrawal from the stress-inducing situation.[3]

Such reluctance suggests a deeper level of brokenness that must be addressed if true unity is to be achieved across racial lines of division. It is likely that similar sets of assumptions, prejudices, and fears across other divides will also have to be addressed if unity is to be our destiny. As people of God, we stand in need of an ongoing, inside-out transformation. This metamorphosis should precede our encounters and carry us into and beyond them. Our growth and transformation must be ongoing if unity is to have a place to sprout among us. Moreover, this transfiguration is one in which we must be fully invested.

I have a habit of describing my workshop space as a "learning zone." I want it to be a place where honest dialogue, engagement with the curriculum, group work, and personal reflection lead the participants to a path of ongoing growth. As I work through the Scriptures, it appears the upper room experience was just such a

---

3. Robin DiAngelo, *White Fragility: Why It Is So Hard for White People to Talk about Racism* (Boston: Beacon, 2018), 2.

time of transformation for the disciples. This formative encounter was situated between their first haltering steps as apprentices of Jesus, and their being charged with the overwhelming task of welcoming the world into the kingdom of God. The upper room encounter was an important breakthrough in the development of their ministry. Gathered in a group, they sought the Lord in prayer. Their understanding of their vocation was expanded, and in that season of new life unity was born among them.

The upper room experience, as it is described in the first chapter of Acts, marks a significant transition moment for the disciples. Whatever happened in that space immediately following the ascension of our Lord appears to have prepared the disciples to engage the diverse world in a posture that was welcoming. In this formative encounter, the disciples shed much of the wrongheaded thinking they so often displayed in the New Testament.

In the Gospel of Luke, the disciples are routinely portrayed in a less than flattering light. Indeed, they miss the mark when it comes to displaying the habits of the heart and mind required for the practice of unity. They turned away children and infants (Luke 18:15), they jockeyed for position (Luke 22:24–30), and they even tried to discourage another follower from carrying out his work simply because he was not a part of their inner group (Luke 9:49). It is hard to see how such a selfish and prideful spirit could have produced unity.

According to the writer of the book of Acts, this early group of disciples was composed of a small cadre of Galileans. During this era the region of Galilee was about twenty-five miles in diameter. Any portion of this area could be reached within a couple of days. Though many of its inhabitants likely were familiar with the Greek language, it was often viewed by those residing in Jerusalem as a "backward locale."[4] The manner in which these disciples

---

4. Rainer Riesner, "Galilee," *Dictionary of Jesus and the Gospels* (Downers Grove, IL: InterVarsity Press, 1992), 253.

were socialized was likely quite similar. They shared a common language, apparently flavored with an accent. They shared similar cultural habits, and they all embraced the same faith tradition. They likely viewed the wider world through a common lens. It is reasonable to assume that this same worldview was marred by a unique set of biases of the type inherent in all cultures.

One might conclude, then, that the followers of Jesus were from the beginning nowhere near being ready to encounter outsiders from different cultures. They would first have to develop the grace and the hospitality required to minister to those who would be coming into the kingdom. Next, they would need to scoot over to allow these same newcomers to be seated at the table of fellowship by the Spirit. It wasn't merely power and boldness these disciples lacked in those early days. They would have to become adept at encountering difference, at meeting others as worthy recipients of God's love. They would have to see them as deserving of God's invitation into the kingdom.

The disciples could have opted for some shortcut, some way around the upper room. They could have taken up the Great Commission unprepared in heart and habits to engage the people groups they would inevitably encounter. This easier route would have allowed them to dodge the kind of reflection, prayer, and practice important in any successful encounter with diversity. In the case of the early disciples, however, the risen Lord would have none of it.

Perhaps it would do no real harm to use a bit of imaginative license when considering what might have occurred among the disciples in the upper room. The writer of Acts tells us they miraculously received the ability to speak in various languages (Acts 2:4). Indeed, this gift was essential, but not sufficient. There in the upper room, the disciples felt their full humanity restored to them. They were given eyes that allowed them to see themselves as God viewed them. In this redeemed state of mind, they looked at others with compassion. Before this formative process came to completion, the assembled group of believers had begun to catch a vision of the kingdom of God, one that included all people. Without such a season of conditioning, it is difficult to imagine how the disciples could have carried out the *missio Dei*.

In these early days the disciples of Jesus learned to embrace the radical equality that was to characterize relations within the community of faith; women and children were to be welcomed, valued, and loved. The disciples had to learn to become comfortable with the idea that not everyone who followed Jesus would make their home among the original twelve. Some, like the apostle Paul, would carry the message of hope beyond the Jewish world. Gentile followers of Jesus would leave off the practice of Jewish religious customs. Diversity within the growing body of Christ multiplied with the addition of each new member.

In the book of Acts, the author illumines the unfolding plan God had set in motion. They would proclaim the good news of Jesus first in Jerusalem, then to areas adjacent to the city, then to Samaria, and finally to the rest of the world (Acts 1:8). The disciples learned to cross borders. In order to meet those whom they would encounter with a proper spirit, they had to overcome their biases toward other Jewish groups, the Samaritans, and finally the unnumbered multitudes of non-Jews. Once these biases were addressed, they would have to stretch some more in order to welcome the group from just over the next hill—beyond the next boundary and border. These newcomers might speak a different tongue; they might exhibit different cultural practices. The disciples were expected nonetheless to adjust and grow. This stretching was a necessary prerequisite to the church's ministry to the world, and it still is expected of believers today.

Before sending the disciples out into a diverse world, our Lord was adamant. His followers were to stay put in Jerusalem until they were visited by the power of God. They needed some time in the upper room under the guidance of the Spirit to get themselves together. There was more to the mission than simply a willingness to travel; they had to prepare their hearts and minds in "continuous and united prayer."[5]

In Acts, prayer offers a backdrop for the kind of intense stretching and preparation that the practice of unity requires. One might consider the apostle Peter's faith journey as a case in point. Before the divine call directed Peter to go down to the house of Cornelius, the apostle went to the housetop to pray (Acts 10:9). It was during this time of prayer, a period of rather intense wrestling with God, that the Lord prepared the apostle to meet his gentile counterpart. Peter was called upon to examine his formation and overcome his prejudices against gentiles. He was almost forced to open his arms to the diversity represented by those gathered in the house of Cornelius.

Once empowered by the Spirit like Peter was, the disciples would be prepared to meet the world as ambassadors of the kingdom. Their message would become matched with the kind of relational posture necessary to give their words credibility. Esteemed Church of God leader James Earl Massey writes:

> Evangelism happens best where love controls the witnessing sharers. . . . It is not hard to make others hear our message if we are close enough to touch them; nor is it difficult to persuade them to believe our message if they see its effects at work in our lives. This explains why Jesus insisted that evangelism proceed only after a full surrender of the self to the Holy Spirit. The love needed to relate to people as a witness is God's gift to the personality. . . . The Holy Spirit helps us match the message we are sent to announce and share. Evangelism demands the right message on the one hand and the right spirit for sharing on the other.[6]

5. I. Howard Marshall, *Acts*, Tyndale New Testament Commentaries (Leicester: Inter-Varsity Press, 1980), 5:62.

6. James Earl Massey, "Culturally Conscious Evangelism," in *Views from the*

The ability to practice unity, to meet others in a loving and respectful manner, is central to God's work. Jesus sent his followers to the upper room to prepare them to be effective in their evangelistic endeavors. Similarly, the preparation leading up to Peter's evangelistic crusade to Cornelius's house reveals the intense stretching and reformation required to get him ready for this diversity encounter. This story involves Peter's wrestling with God over how he was trained to think about non-Jews and Romans. In those moments God revealed the inherent evil present in Peter's biases and prejudices, obstacles hindering Peter's work as a disciple.

The shape of God's plan came into focus slowly for Peter. Perhaps because it was such a new idea for him. In this transformative moment he heard the Lord telling him, "Do not call anything impure that God has made clean" (Acts 10:15). Later, after he had some time to mull over the episode, he simply would say that he had come to understand he "should not call anyone impure or unclean" (Acts 10:28). This above passage mapping Peter's preparation to carry the gospel to the non-Jews shows that the cognitive dissonance that this episode occasioned in Peter was not so easy to digest. Nor was this spirit of oneness always maintained by the apostle.

According to the New Testament record, none other than the apostle Paul subsequently challenged Peter because the latter had stopped eating with his gentile counterparts after a Jewish delegation arrived at the church in Antioch (Galatians 2:11–14). This duplicity angered Paul. Perhaps viewing Peter's struggle with prejudice through the lens of these two texts allows us to get some sense of how difficult it is to root out this kind of malformation.

The link between evangelism and the practice of unity is important for believers committed to oneness in today's church.

Mountain: Select Writings of James Earl Massey, ed. Barry L. Callen and Curtiss P. DeYoung (Marion, IN: Aldersgate, 2018), 221.

More recent attempts to spread the gospel have provided the impetus for some of the more developed initiatives promoting church unity. For example, a commitment to John Paul II's "new evangelization" program serves as a driving force behind the creation of the intercultural training initiative created by the United States Conference of Catholic Bishops' Committee on Cultural Diversity in the Church. This "new evangelization" takes on unity-bursting trends in the United States such as secularism, individualism, and materialism. It further aims to see the gospel spread in areas previously evangelized but presently showing signs of falling away. Undergirding this effort is the 1975 apostolic exhortation *Evangelii Nuntiandi* by Pope Paul VI. Four pillars of evangelization can be identified from this source, including

1. conversion: imagined as a personal encounter with Jesus Christ;
2. the evangelization of cultures: taking into account a people's rituals, symbols, and myths (narratives) as well as the gospel, a process leading to the transformation of culture (inculturation);
3. liberation: promoted as the transformation of social, economic, and political orders in light of the gospel values of life and human dignity; and
4. ecumenical and interreligious dialogue: with the goal of bringing about the unity of all peoples in pursuit of Jesus's mandate.[7]

Popes John Paul II, Benedict XVI, and Francis have referred to the church as "missionary in its entirety." A natural result of such a focus is the acquisition of the "intercultural knowledge, skills and attitudes that enable ministers of the Gospel to pro-

---

7. United States Conference of Catholic Bishops Committee on Cultural Diversity in the Church, *Building Intercultural Competence for Ministers* (Washington, DC: United States Conference of Catholic Bishops, 2012), 2.

claim Christ's message effectively among all nations."[8] It is just these sorts of skills and sensitivities that an upper room–like encounter has the potential to develop.

A Return to the Upper Room

The past few years in ministry have felt different for me. It seems like the church is intensely divided across a number of fronts. Hateful attitudes once forced underground by a collective sense of civility have resurfaced with a vengeance. Christians following the rest of society have chosen sides, identified enemies, and at times declared war on their sisters and brothers who hold differing political affiliations. Divides over contentious social and moral issues are also fortified by elements within the body of Christ. "They are either with us or against us," seems to be today's mantra.

The 2016 election further intensified such divides, and this is nowhere more apparent than in the schism between white Christians and Christians of color. This shift in race relations in the aftermath of the 2016 election has been noted by Daniel Hill:

> The already-present racial divide in the church became further enflamed by the election, and it manifested in some concrete ways. That divide was on display in the betrayal and anger many Christians of color communicated toward white Christians. Some of the respected bridge-building leaders went so far as to publicly question whether there could ever be genuine unity across racial lines in the American church.
>
> On the other side were white Christians, many of them displaying shock at the outrage from their brothers and sis-

8. Committee on Cultural Diversity in the Church, *Building Intercultural Competence*, 5.

ters of color. To them the election was about something very different from race, and they were perplexed about why the results had landed so hard on people of color. What became clear to everyone during this time was that regardless of where one's political views landed, the result was that the racial breach between Christians had grown qualitatively worse.[9]

Other voices communicated their dismay and hurt over the results of the 2016 election. More important, their responses reveal a disconnect between how whites and people of color viewed the culmination of this watershed political campaign. Novelist Attica Locke described this sentiment in a radio interview: "I was so profoundly hurt to realize that there were still so many people in the country [who] were fine electing someone who said such hateful things about people who look like me just because it made economic sense to them. I don't know what to do with that, and I'm still wrestling with forgiveness. I don't know how or if to forgive."[10]

As designated evangelists and practitioners of unity, the account of the upper room offers contemporary followers of Jesus hope for transformation. In a divided world plagued by cultural ignorance and willful divisiveness, a more robust upper room theology accompanied by a set of practices designed to facilitate growth might help believers get back on track. Inundated by the Holy Spirit in such a learning environment, it might be possible to recapture a vision of the united church, one whose members come from every tribe, tongue, nation, class grouping, and culture. Gathered together in prayer and the practice of unity, the "still small voice" might then possess the bandwidth to drown

9. Hill, *White Awake*, 34–35.

10. Attica Locke, "In 'Heaven My Home' Attica Locke Shows a Part of Texas We Don't Usually See," interview by Sam Briger, *Fresh Air*, NPR, October 16, 2019, https://www.npr.org/2019/10/16/770613459/in-heaven-my-home-attica -locke-shows-a-part-of-texas-we-don-t-usually-see.

out all that hateful rhetoric and divisive misinformation being disseminated at every turn—even on "Christian radio." Motivated by the greatest commandment, the upper room is the place where we can engage God, our broken selves, and diverse others in meaningful dialogue. Here, in this sacred place, all things can become new (2 Corinthians 5:17).

Practicing Unity in the Upper Room

Make no mistake about it. The divine gift of the Spirit readied the disciples to go out and share the message of the faith. But how are we to understand the role played by the Spirit? Inside those walls the disciples ate together, fellowshipped, talked to one another, and they prayed. This season of preparation allowed them to practice among themselves *the unity within reach*. Here women and men gathered—a zealot, a Roman collaborator, and a few fishermen sat listening to one another. They each learned to value the other. It was a time of marked growth. God was present in every moment of this transfiguration, but so were the followers. The upper room experience was as mundane as it was miraculous, as ordinary as it was wondrous, as human as it was divine.

Eventually, these disciples emerged from their retreat. They had stretched and been stretched in ways previously unimaginable. But the growth was meant to be carried beyond this setting. The unity they learned to practice in the upper room would subsequently be drawn on to welcome outsiders into the kingdom. And after all this prayer and practice, then came the Holy Spirit sealing them for this boundary-bursting work.

The church today at times feels like it is situated somewhere between the ascension and Pentecost. Perhaps what we need is to return to the upper room in order to relearn how to relate across the divides that separate sister from brother. God will meet us there, yet we have a part to play as well. Below I propose some initial elements of a curriculum for this season of growth.

In such a curriculum one might give more focus to:

1. The church's mandate to carry the message of the gospel to the diverse world. This would include how the Bible and church teaching support such a mission.
2. Deepening the study of demographics. Such research might address questions like "What are the unique cultural characteristics of the community?" "What challenges do its inhabitants face?" and "How might the church meet the pressing needs of these individuals and groups?"
3. The process of socialization—in other words, how individuals learn to see the world as they do. A critique of the positive and negative aspects of this societal formation.
4. The mastery of terms associated with the study of intercultural ministry.
5. A push to improve intercultural competence.
6. A general review of the history of one's particular denomination or faith community with an eye toward the times when unity was practiced well, as well as times when group members missed the mark in this regard.
7. The challenges (internal and external) that tend to work against the experience of genuine community.
8. Sexism, racism, homophobia, xenophobia, and other forms of bigotry, particularly the resulting impact each might have on the church.

The upper room is empty and waiting to be visited by members of today's church. I'm not sure that we must wait for specific instructions from the Lord to head that way. We need only be fired by a love of God and neighbor. In the next chapter, we will discuss how the Bible can be used either to thwart or encourage us in this important unity-building work.

Upper Room Exercises

Reflection

Much of the hurt we experience when negotiating difference is related to the unhealthy ways we see ourselves and others. Reflect on a time when you felt like someone misjudged or devalued you in a hurtful manner. Do you recall an incident when you offended someone else in a similar way?

Questions for Discussion

1. Have you ever experienced an upper room–type encounter? Share it with the class.
2. Cite evidence showing that your church might reap benefits from a return to the upper room.
3. Which of the upper room curriculum suggestions would be the most beneficial to you or your church? Explain.
4. What role has prayer played in your spiritual growth? How has devotion to this discipline improved your practice of unity?

From Pew to Practice

Speculate as to the reason novelist Attica Locke was aggrieved at her white sisters and brothers. Learn about four or five critical issues of concern to voters of color. Share what you discover with others.

Chapter Five

The Bible and the Practice of Unity

When we read the Bible poorly, we are at risk of allowing it to pull us earthward toward our baser instincts. We then find within its pages what we hoped we would. We discover a justification for building walls, vilifying fellow citizens, or labeling those who oppose our politics and moral positions as "enemies." It is all laid out before us in letters fixed to page.

Though there are marked differences regarding how to interpret the Bible, it nonetheless holds a central place and normative function in the lives of Christians. In its pages one finds instructions that promote the practice of unity—instances in the Bible where peacemaking, reconciliation, and harmonious relations are encouraged. Yet we also read of conflict, fighting, war, schism, and disunity. Because the Bible has authority among the faithful, people embracing a wide variety of opinions have claimed it as an ally. Well-meaning and benevolent folk have searched its contents in order to promote peace, justice, and equitable relations. On the other hand, this same set of texts has been used just as often to foment fear, distrust, and anger. These more problematic interpretations (in my view) have in turn led to conflict, schism, oppression, genocide, and war.

Promoters of unity need only look to the New Testament letters attributed to Paul to find evidence of the Bible's support of unity and oneness. In his letter to the church at Ephesus, Paul illumines God's grand plan "to be put in effect when the times reach their fulfillment." This plan according to the apostle is "to bring unity to all things in heaven and on earth under Christ" (Ephesians 1:10). Paul calls on his readers to practice this unity; they are to be "completely humble and gentle . . . patient, bearing with one another in love." Moreover, they are encouraged to "make every effort to keep the unity of the Spirit through the bond of peace" (Ephesians 4:2–3). The oneness of the body of Christ is to be in no way compromised by the varied gifts divinely bestowed on the members of the church (Ephesians 4:9–13). Finally, the Christians in Ephesus are directed to walk in "the way of love" (Ephesians 5:2). The theme of this epistle makes it a suitable primer for believers seeking to live in oneness.

Paul's first letter to the Corinthian church also provides a biblical foundation for understanding the theme of unity. In his first recorded correspondence to this church, the apostle pleads that his readers come together: "I appeal to you, brothers and sisters, in the name of our Lord Jesus Christ, that all of you agree with one another in what you say and that there be no divisions among you, but that you be perfectly united in mind and thought" (1 Corinthians 1:10).

In examining select passages in the New Testament to discover how they function in the promotion of genuine unity, I make use of a "hermeneutic of inclusion." That is, I aim to read these passages as if the text's focus on unity matters and that we are meant to embody oneness as a witness before our broken and fragmented world. I take up the Bible with the knowledge that Jesus practiced radical inclusivity. He transgressed the boundaries between women and men, children and rulers, saints and sinners. This approach to the Bible assumes the reality of God's kingdom and the continuing echo of the universal invitation:

"Let the one who wishes take the free gift of the water of life" (Revelation 22:17).

One temptation attending this hermeneutical method may be to act as if we are the keepers of the kingdom of God—that we set its parameters and mind its gates. Let me state at the outset, then, that my approach to unity and inclusion acknowledges that the entity we welcome others into is not under our jurisdiction or control. In other words, the kingdom is neither mine nor yours to define. Rather, we are called to be inclusive on our generous Lord's account. This habit of hospitality is mandated for every other believer who joins us as well.

Leaning on a long line of biblical interpreters, I refuse to see the text's ethical directives as frozen forever in time. The Bible itself encourages believers in our generation to push forward, struggle, think, and discover more clearly God's path for us. It requires people today to stretch as much in service of unity and inclusion as it did the disciples of old. I see the Bible as both relevant and demanding for divided people today. Its insight propels the family of faith on a trajectory that will lead us to embrace an ever-widening field of diverse people, all seeking to walk in the light of God. Scripture must not, however, be weaponized by those who would divide. Nor should it be employed to encourage us to cover our ears against the Spirit who makes the message intelligible in every tongue and in each generation.

Reading the Bible through a hermeneutic of inclusion exposes instances of division and injustice in the text. When one reads the text with inclusion as the interpretive key, one sees the full scope of villainy in the actions of those who sow mistrust and discord. Take, for example, the narrative account of Paul and Silas's missionary journey to the city of Philippi (Acts 16:16–40). While there, the two missionaries attempt to establish a new church. In the process, however, they end up threatening an economic enterprise operated by a number of the city's merchants, an enterprise that was exploiting a young girl. When the business leaders sought to silence Paul and Silas, they did so by stoking anti-Semitic sentiments. This divisive action comes into stark focus when reading this passage through a lens of inclusion.

A Personal Note on Reading the Bible Inclusively

My attraction to a hermeneutic of inclusion began at an early age. I grew up in a congregation that emphasized the importance of Bible reading. As a young man I took on a regimen that included one hour of reading per day. Following this plan I was able to read the New Testament through thirteen times in one year. Yet as I look back at the fruit of my early Bible reading, I am disturbed by a heartlessness coupled with a fairly developed sense of spiritual superiority. This lethal combination distorted my reading of the sacred text, so my devotional reading did not always inspire the generosity of spirit required for the practice of unity.

During this formative time, I recall making a trip with our youth group to another state in order to visit a Christian college. On our free day, we decided to visit a local beach. As we were enjoying our time together, we were joined by a busty middle-aged woman who was obviously inebriated. She stopped to talk for a bit, but I made a demeaning joke about her as the group urged me on. As it turned out, all that Bible reading had not prepared me to receive this woman's friendliness toward us. I considered her less than. I knew lots of Bible verses, but clearly something was missing.

Oddly enough, it was not until I put the Bible down and began to read other books that I began to grow as a Christian. It was only then that my heart opened to hear stories of those whose life experiences and perspectives were different from my own. Their dreams, aspirations, and pain came into view with each turn of the page. I looked beyond the borders of my own tradition in order to observe how others lived their lives. What motivated them? What interested them? What did they see that I couldn't? The accumulated insight helped me to hear the message of the Bible in new ways—that is, I began to read through a lens of inclusion.

I began to experience the Bible through the eyes of others. My reading partners were my diverse sisters and brothers, the living and the dead, believers as well as critics of organized religion. Some were part of the LGBTQ community, and others were often dismissed as feminists and revolutionaries. But we read the Bible in community, thereby countering the tendency to interpret its message in ways that reinforce our heartlessness and dangerous prejudices.

We read the Bible well when folks from other demographics open its pages with us. Making use of the collective insight of a diverse interpretive family allows the book to speak prophetically to us. When reading this way, we should prepare ourselves to hear the voice of the divine.

The meaning my diverse sisters and brothers drew from the Bible was very different from my own gleanings. Where I saw personal salvation and the need to live a holy and sanctified life, they saw liberation and societal transformation. Where I celebrated instances in which charity was extended, they emphasized the need for justice. No doubt, growth was taking place; I could feel it. When I returned to the Bible in my times of quiet reflection, I would do so with very different eyes.

READING WITH A LENS OF INCLUSION

We in the church might benefit from a little therapy when it comes to our relationship to the Bible. It seems some purposeful discussion around the assumptions we bring to the text, as well as the question of what we expect from it, would be profitable. We shouldn't, for example, expect it to do all our thinking for us. Nor should we expect it to drown out all the insight bequeathed to members of the body of Christ. Moreover, it cannot be permitted to make us less generous, grace-filled, loving, patient, and kind.

At times, the Bible becomes just another instrument to be used for our own ends. The multitude of voices from within pointing us to the good and to the way of integrity under God too often go unheard. In a world where many of our associations are transactional, it might surprise no one that our relationship to the Bible would reflect this same brokenness. Rather than coming to the text with a posture of openness to real and meaningful exchange, we too often come with an agenda. We are so accustomed to approaching the Bible this way we hardly even notice it as problematic. We read to improve our lives; we read to learn how to get ahead; we read to better manage our finances, our marriages, or our careers. In other words, we commodify the Bible—we come to it, get we want, and then go.

When we read the Bible poorly, we are at risk of allowing it to pull us toward our baser instincts. We then find within its pages what we hoped we would. We discover a justification for building walls, vilifying fellow citizens, or labeling those who oppose our politics and moral positions as "enemies." It is all laid out before us in letters fixed to page.

Equally problematic, I suppose, is our tendency to view the Bible writers as more tuned in to God than the faithful of our own generation. In so doing we run the risk of creating the kind of hierarchy Jesus seemed so bent on deconstructing. Indeed, we today as believers may have more insight than our pious forebears on various matters related to the kingdom. We must not discount these fresh deposits of wisdom and insight simply because of our inherent, albeit misguided, tendency to elevate some above others. Hierarchy works against unity.

Our aim, then, is to learn to be led by the Spirit giving space so the writers of the Bible can cheer us on rather than hold us up. The text certainly is our guiding light, but we dare not forget the important role every generation of believers must play in the process of discerning. Instead, we will rely on the Spirit and the generous deposit of gifts and sensitivities bestowed on God's children of every generation. The Bible is not a book held in trusteeship by a self-recognized few, but rather it belongs to believers dispersed as they are in the many camps comprising the diverse family of faith. Learning to read it in community, without privileging some voices over others, is our work. Such an ongoing interdependence is itself a product of the unity of the body of Christ.

Christians who are committed to the faithful practice of unity must tend their interpretations of Scripture with prayerful watchfulness, in part because the Bible has so often been used to shore up oppressive systems. In his important book, *Jesus and the Disinherited*, Howard Thurman relates how such a distorted presentation of the Bible impacted his grandmother, who suffered the violence of slavery. Because of her position she was not permitted to learn to read or write.

When Thurman was a young boy, his grandmother asked him to read the Bible for her. In these sessions she permitted him to read only certain parts of the Scripture. After completing a couple of years of college, he questioned his grandmother as to why she never asked him to read from the Pauline corpus. During her years of servitude, she explained, her former owner wouldn't let an African American minister lead their church meetings. Instead, the white slave owner's minister would intermittently hold services. She told Thurman that he exclusively used the writings of Paul. Moreover, he regularly selected these same texts to justify enslavement. In these gatherings the assembled servants were instructed to be "good" and "happy" slaves in order that God might bless them. This experience led his grandmother to promise herself if freedom ever came and she learned how to read, she would refuse to read those used by the white preacher.[1]

---

1. Howard Thurman, *Jesus and the Disinherited* (1949; repr., Boston: Beacon Press, 1996), 20.

Those who read the Bible through a lens of inclusion must prepare to discover fresh insight from its pages. The knowledge that the Holy Spirit continues the work of bringing believers into step with God's designs must be kept at the forefront of our thinking. Episcopal bishop Gene Robinson shares a similar insight:

> The changes we've seen in our understanding of scripture over the nineteen centuries since it was written have happened through the guidance of the Holy Spirit. . . .
>
> This is good news for Christians. God didn't stop revealing God's self with the closing of the canon of scripture. God is still actively engaged in ongoing revelation over time, even in our own day. God didn't just "inspire" the scriptures to be written and then walk away, wishing us well in our attempts to understand those words. God's Holy Spirit continues to lead us into all the truth, as Jesus promised on the night before he was betrayed.[2]

Many Bible passages assume a developmental understanding of God's work in the world. On one occasion, for example, Jesus said to his followers, "I have much more to say to you, more than you can now bear. But when he, the Spirit of truth, comes, he will guide you into all the truth. He will not speak on his own; he will speak only what he hears, and he will tell you what is yet to come" (John 16:12–13). Rather than one big deposit of insight to sustain the disciples for all time and in all circumstances, they would instead be given understanding as they were able to digest it. Like an elementary student studying under the direction of an instructor, elements of God's curriculum are disclosed at just the right time. One factor in the timing of these deposits of insight is no doubt the maturity of God's people.

---

2. Gene Robinson, *In the Eye of Storm: Swept to the Center by God* (New York: Seabury Books, 2008), 59.

Each succeeding generation and every community has a part to play in discerning God's will and way in this world. Through prayer, abiding in the Spirit, and walking in communion with our sisters and brothers, God's fount of knowledge is available, helping us to recognize how the Scriptures promote fullness of life in a particular time and place. The apostle Peter was a recipient of this ongoing enlightenment when he discerned that the gentiles were also destined to become full citizens of the kingdom of God. Similarly, this same type of insight lifted Paul, who came to see (at least partially) how the institution of slavery compromised the radical equality promoted by followers of Jesus. Over the succeeding two millennia, this light has illumined more clearly our way forward, opening up new vistas, illumining new fields of enterprise, and helping the followers of Christ work in partnership with the Spirit.

Best-selling author Preston Sprinkle speaks about how previously firm church traditions have shifted over time as believers grew in their collective understanding of God's will and way. For example, the institutional church changed its mind regarding its condemnation of Galileo's view of the cosmos. Similarly, in the nineteenth century, the church moved away from its support of the institution of slavery. On a more personal level, Sprinkle writes about his own shifting views regarding the ethics of the use of military force. Much to his own surprise, he came to embrace absolute nonviolence as the more principled Christian alternative.[3]

The practice of unity is complicated by conflicting interpretations of the Bible. Compromising these same convictions for the sake of "keeping the peace" for many is simply an inappropriate course of action. On the other hand, there are individuals who feel their very dignity is threatened by the way these same

3. Preston Sprinkle, *People to Be Loved: Why Homosexuality Is Not Just an Issue* (Grand Rapids: Zondervan, 2015), 18.

principled people interpret the sacred text. The issue of marriage equality and LGBTQ rights poses a seemingly intractable dilemma in many churches and denominations, leading to a breakdown of unity.

The fact that disunity exists, that complex divisions threaten to divide the body of Christ, should shift us all into a unity-promoting mode. We should slow down and proceed carefully in prayerful watchfulness. The prospect of division necessitates a period of thoughtful and ongoing reflection as to how the Bible, the traditions, and the resources of the church are being used to buttress one side of the argument or another. In addition, elements of the following oneness-promoting protocol might also come into play:

1. Prioritize unity at whatever level seems best for the entire community.
2. Commit to slowing the process of separation, giving time for cooler heads to prevail.
3. Enter a period of structured listening, one which allows all parties to be respected and heard.
4. Throughout this time of intentional discernment maintain a learning posture.
5. If parting must occur, it should be done without curses and anathemas.
6. Keep the door of fellowship, dialogue, and cooperation open at the most comprehensive level possible.

When reading the Bible with an eye toward unity and inclusion, it is possible to see elements of our theological heritage in a new light. One important biblical theme given a new emphasis as a result of this reading approach is the experience of salvation and new birth. Reading key passages, which will be examined below, through this lens of inclusion illumines how the new birth experience relates to the practice of reconciliation toward the alienated other. When we experience conversion to God it concurrently impacts our human relationships, particularly those that are broken. Our willingness to turn to God in a posture of love, as in genuine conversion, must always be mirrored in our relationships with the neglected or despised other.

Getting right with God can't be divorced from the need to be reconciled with those in our relational network—not only those we have wronged, but also those who have injured us. Reading the Bible through a lens of inclusion helps us to see that the new birth experience must be more thickly defined. It sets us right with others as well as with God. When we are reconciled to God we are necessarily moving in the direction of our unreconciled sisters and brothers. Baptism brings us into a community of oneness. When we act in accordance with this grace, broken relationships are set right, and divisive labels lose their hold on us. Indeed, "There is neither Jew nor Gentile, neither slave nor free, nor is there male and female." We are instead "all one in Christ Jesus" (Galatians 3:28).

When viewed through the lens of inclusion, the story of the reconciliation of Zacchaeus (Luke 19:1–10) allows us to see how conversion and the experience of salvation have implications beyond one's relationship to God. Zacchaeus was a tax collector. His willingness to work for the Roman occupiers, therefore, likely made him a *persona non grata*. The resentment directed toward him in this account is understandable. Given the lifestyle of this tax collector, it is no wonder that coming to God would necessarily involve the victims he had defrauded.

Zacchaeus's unorthodox attempt to see Jesus was matched by the Lord's desire to seek out lost souls. Jesus engaged Zacchaeus. He called him by name, and then invited himself to the tax collector's home for lodging. In making this invitation, Jesus gave Zacchaeus the chance to receive not only God's messenger, but also the good news of the kingdom of God.[4] A miracle in the life of Zacchaeus began with a border crossing.

The conversion of Zacchaeus was about more than simply one repentant sinner. Indeed, the wayward and misguided tax gatherer felt the warm embrace of God in the person of Jesus. Yet this was no mere "God and me" moment. Rather, this conversion impacted those who knew Zacchaeus, including the people who were victims of his extortion, the poor who suffered under the Roman occupation. Salvation is not merely about getting one's soul right with God. It rather calls us to unity, to reconciliations across all of our networks of relationships. This restoration of human relationships around Zacchaeus was integral to the salvation he experienced on that day. In summary, conversion for Zacchaeus was more than a crisis moment, more than a trip to the mourner's bench, more than coming to know a "personal savior"; rather, it was a reconciliation with both God and God's vulnerable children. Moreover, his salvation was linked to the amelioration of injustice and economic oppression in his community.

Allan Aubrey Boesak brings into clearer focus the horizontal (human to human) dimension of reconciliation when he brings the story of Zacchaeus's conversion into dialogue with his groundbreaking work on reconciliation in South Africa. Conversion was not merely a matter related to the tax gatherer's heart. Boesak writes:

> Zacchaeus drew radical conclusions from his conversion and the act of being reconciled with God. He knew this reconciliation needed to be effected with the community in order for it to be genuine. He understood that reconciliation has to mean transformation if it is to mean anything: of his life and

---

4. Luke Timothy Johnson, *Sacra Pagina: The Gospel of Luke* (Collegeville, MN: Liturgical Press, 1991), 3:285.

lifestyle, his relationships with the community, and especially with those he had wronged. Zacchaeus knew that reconciliation means the restoration of justice, relationships, dignity, integrity, and human fulfillment.[5]

How different our interpersonal relationships might be if the church's understanding of the conversion experience included a requisite realignment of our broken relationships. The communal results would even be more impactful if this understanding were wed to Boesak's insight about the costliness of reconciliation.[6]

When read through the lens of inclusion, the story of the conversion of Saul also yields insight on the relationship between the experience of rebirth or salvation and the promotion of unity. When the reader first meets Saul, he has been violently targeting Jesus's followers.

Though the account doesn't reveal the finer details of Saul's errant thinking, it is safe to say that he looked on himself and those who believed as he did to be protectors of the truth. Despite the similarities between the early believers of Jesus and those who practiced Saul's brand of Judaism, he believed these heretics had to be eliminated.

Saul was already blinded by his hatred and bigotry long before his blinding experience on the road to Damascus. When Saul encountered the Lord on that memorable day, he was also destined to meet a community of believers who up to that time he had despised. The Lord and the persecuted minority were together. The process of conversion would be more than successful completion of a new church member's class. Rather, Saul underwent a radical reorientation to God as well as a decisive turning away from the malice he harbored against the followers of Jesus.

---

5. Curtiss Paul DeYoung, *Coming Together in the 21st Century: The Bible's Message in an Age of Diversity* (Valley Forge, PA: Judson Press, 2009), 146.

6. DeYoung, *Coming Together*, 146.

Conversion included a horizontal dimension as well. In this God encounter, no dark corner of Saul's heart would be undisturbed, and no hostile relationship unaddressed. His conversion was so complete, it necessitated a name change; Saul became Paul.

But Saul's conversion was far from over when he was helped back to his feet after meeting Jesus. It was as if the Lord had pulled a cruel joke on the pious fundamentalist. Saul's conversion would necessarily be aided by a representative of the very group he had so heartlessly sought to stamp out. The comical irony of the situation is hard to miss. The future apostle was not only dependent on God's mercy, but he was also similarly at the mercy of this beleaguered community of faith. He needed them in order to be healed of his blindness and his bigotry. In the end, Saul's journey to God through conversion led him straight through a fellowship of believers which had before been the object of his hate. Conversion for Saul meant a radical reorientation to them as well as to God.

But Saul was not the only one in this narrative who had to change. The divine plan to bring Saul into the early church also required a good deal of stretching on the part of the community of Jesus followers. Ananias, who seems to have been a member rather than a leader of the group, represents in his actions the entire fellowship. His dramatic encounter with the Lord seems no less miraculous than Saul's Damascus road meeting. In his mystical encounter, the disciple is told to go find Saul, this archenemy of his people. Ananias is then charged with healing his blindness and praying over the future saint in order that he might receive the Holy Spirit (Acts 9:11–17).

Ananias's decision to go to Saul took grace and not a small portion of courage. He was privy to Saul's violent reputation (Acts 9:13–14). Perhaps some in the Christian community thought Saul to be unredeemable. Yet Ananias believed that he himself was called to act as a healing agent and then as an evangelist for the future saint. When he arrived in the place where this former enemy of the church was staying, Ananias showed his radical commitment to the practice of unity. He stretched out his hand in fellowship, and "Brother Saul," was his greeting. Indeed, as Saul would come to learn later, the community of faith was enlivened by this familial spirit. Despite his violent reputation, Saul was welcomed into the fellowship. Saul became a new person when the community of Jesus followers embraced him; the fledgling church had also been transformed as it opened its trembling arms to one who had attempted to stamp it out. Only later would it become clear that in Saul they had found a champion.

Another gospel account found in Acts, when read through a lens of inclusion, illumines a more comprehensive view of conversion, one that emphasizes one's restoration not only to God but also to individuals in the convert's relational orbit. In the account of the conversion of the Macedonian jailer, the experience of salvation changed the jailer's relationship to God, yes, but it also restored his relationship to Paul and Silas, who had been mistreated and abused by the civic establishment he himself belonged to (Acts 16:19–24).

Paul and Silas came to the region of Macedonia in response to a divine vision (Acts 16:9–10). The fellowship established from this divinely directed endeavor appears to have been diverse from the start. The group met in the home of Lydia, a wealthy seller of purple cloth (Acts 16:15). As the church grew, it appears to have modeled the diversity of the populace living in the surrounding region. The unnamed young girl who had been trafficked by her owners would have found a home within the fellowship, as would the Philippian jailer following his dramatic conversion. This was a faith community committed to the practice of unity. In short, the divisions of wealth and social status were not permitted to tier or otherwise divide those joining the group.

As Paul and Silas made their way into to the city of Philippi under the Spirit's direction, they carried with them the message of the gospel. Whether they initially received a warm reception is unknown. We do know they ministered in this locale for some time before running afoul of the local authorities (Acts 16:12). The episode landing Paul and Silas in the Philippian jail began when Paul cast a spirit out of a troubled young woman with a clairvoyant capability. This same individual had been in bondage to a group of merchant handlers. The apostle's decision to heal this woman rendered her useless to the ones who were exploiting this power for their own enrichment. Angered by this loss of revenue, the woman's exploiters ginned up anti-Jewish sentiment against Paul and Silas (Acts 16:16–21). This religious prejudice is what was stirred up in opposition to the work these ministers were conducting. Luke Timothy Johnson writes, "To the pagan purveyors of prophecy, they [Paul and Silas] appear to be Jews, and the dormant antisemitic tendencies of the urban rabble are quickly incited by the xenophobic charges brought against the apostles by the complainants."[7]

The enslavers whose economic prospects were damaged by the missionary enterprise decided Paul and Silas had to go. In order to create a hostile atmosphere, they selected a strategy that has worked well across the centuries, vilifying individuals from outside one's social or religious grouping. They stoked the crowd with their claims that Paul and Silas were disruptive outsiders. The crowd took the bait, assaulting the two missionaries. Suffering at the hands of the citizens of Philippi, Paul and Silas were then jailed (Acts 16:20–23). The stripes they received were the direct result of the religious prejudice fanned into flame by those who accused the apostles of bringing foreign customs into the community.

It isn't clear whether the jailer in Philippi had any contact with the two apostles prior to their being delivered to him. Nor does the text tell us whether the jailer wielded the whip to beat the apostles. In any case, he was part of the regime that abused these men. It was he who was charged with locking them up and securing them for future judgement (Acts 16:23–24). Though he

7. Luke Timothy Johnson, *Sacra Pagina: The Acts of the Apostles* (Collegeville, MN: Liturgical Press, 1992), 5:254.

may not have acted violently toward them, he was still a part of a system that brutalized these two well-meaning missionaries.

The scars marking these missionaries' backs did not prevent them from presenting a vibrant witness to those who had been jailed in this same community. On the night of their arrest, they sang praises to God. The prisoners heard their songs (Acts 16:25). Such a remarkable witness made an impression. In the end the jailer experienced a dramatic conversion.

It appears that when conversion came to the jailer, his relationships to God and to Paul and Silas were put in right order. Evidence of this transformation is obvious. He took the two maligned apostles and opened his own home to them. We then witness the jailer washing the wounds on their backs.

Religious bigotry had placed the scars on their backs. But the converted jailer was now dressing these painful wounds, washing the broken flesh and laboring to relieve the pain. The jailer was now a convert, a reconciler, an agent of healing. Washing the wounds of Paul and Silas was a tangible gesture consistent with his conversion. At this juncture the jailer and his household submitted to baptism and became a part of this new, diverse, and radically inclusive community.

The practice of unity involves the promotion of the grace that we see in such passages of Scripture. It is important, however, that this same message be guarded lest a false gospel—one leading to division and discord—be substituted for it. In the next chapter, we will discuss this worrisome topic.

UPPER ROOM EXERCISES

Reflection

Think about your relationship to the Bible. Is it a good one? What can you do to make your relationship to the Bible more meaningful?

Questions for Discussion

1. Which was the most challenging insight presented in this chapter? Explain your answer.

2. Finish the following sentence: We read the Bible well when we _____.

3. Reexamine the conversion accounts from Scripture covered in this chapter, and compare a contemporary conversion account to one of them. What similarities do you see? What differences?

4. If you were afforded the opportunity to speak with Howard Thurman's grandmother, what might you say about how Scripture should be used?

5. How might including a more diverse group of believers into one's reading community enrich the Bible-reading experience?

From Pew to Practice

All of us read the Bible through given interpretive lenses. Take a few minutes to examine the lens through which you read the Bible. Note the theological tradition, church affiliation, and cultural factors shaping your thinking on how it should be interpreted. Seek out an individual from a diverse community and ask them to share about their approach to reading the Bible.

Chapter Six

False Gospels

*In the realm of morals the role of Christianity has been, at best,
ambivalent. . . . If the concept of God has any validity or any use,
it can only be to make us larger, freer, and more loving. If God
cannot do this then it is time we got rid of him.*

—James Baldwin

In the letter to the Galatians, Paul writes to the fledgling church
he had established in that region. He expressed his astonishment that some had been led to embrace a false gospel by those
perverting its message (Galatians 1:6–7). Such a warning echoes
across the centuries down to us as believers today; we must be no
less vigilant regarding the sort of gospel we embrace.

Over the course of the last few years, I have come to question the character of the gospel being promoted in many of our
churches. As elements of the church with which I am engaged
have partnered with political operatives, we have become angrier,
more fearful of outsiders, and more distrustful of those who
hold different political views. And though our engagement in
politics, in the minds of some, has produced fruit, it has not been
without cost.

As we aggressively forged alliances in order to "Christianize"
and otherwise shape society along the lines of our theological con-

victions, we too have been changed. In the process of promoting our interests over against the more vulnerable demographics among us, the gospel has become sullied. Many now wonder whether the church has traded its very soul for a few Supreme Court appointments and the closing of yet another abortion clinic.

The good news—that Jesus came to release the captive, give sight to the blind, proclaim hope to the poor—has become distorted with hard-line immigration rhetoric and policy proposals that make life more difficult for the most financially vulnerable. In many sections of the church it is difficult to distinguish between the gospel of hope on the one hand and a conservative or liberal party platform on the other. The tendency to tailor the gospel to fit a political agenda is but one way the gospel becomes distorted. Cheryl Sanders, a prominent pastor within my movement, writes of this inclination: "Many Christian leaders in America are cutting and pasting the gospel to make it fit in with the worst of our social values and political ideologies, in a mass appeal to greed and selfishness."[1]

It is often easier to see distortions in the gospel message when we look back at previous historical periods. Take, for example, the problematic character of the gospel promoted by Pope Urban II in the eleventh century, who called for a crusade against Muslims in the Holy Land. Similarly, in the mid-twentieth century, the gospel of the Nazi church in Germany was one that capitulated to Adolf Hitler and the Third Reich. Though Christians during this period certainly understood such accommodation to the dictates of this violent and authoritarian regime was illegitimate, an astounding number of believers found no contradiction between a gospel of love and the Nazi policies of hate.

The temptation to tailor the gospel for one's own ends knows no historical or geographic bounds. Early settlers of the United

1. Cheryl J. Sanders, *Ministry at the Margins: The Prophetic Mission of Women, Youth & the Poor* (Downers Grove, IL: InterVarsity Press, 1997), 29.

States claimed the covenant of a promised land for Abraham as their own, displacing indigenous "pagan" peoples while identifying with the military forces of Joshua. And for many years in the United States, the good news of Jesus was somehow consistent with the ownership and trafficking of human beings. As abolitionists raised religious arguments against slaveholders, the latter doubled down, even invoking both testaments to support the "peculiar institution."

One of the most notorious defenses of slavery was the curse of Ham. According to this theory, after the great flood Noah cursed his youngest son Ham for looking on his nakedness. As part of this curse, Ham's son Canaan was doomed to serve as a slave to Noah's other sons, Shem and Japheth. Over time, the curse came to be associated with those of African descent, which Christian slaveholders were only too willing to believe—and exploit.[2]

The New Testament also was used to support a gospel sanctioning human slavery. Southern ministers routinely argued that Jesus never explicitly condemned the practice. After all, they argued, he had the opportunity when he healed the centurion's servant's ear (Luke 7:1–10), so why did he not take the occasion to denounce such service to begin with?[3] Such readings of course push the boundaries of sound interpretation, but they were popular nonetheless.

And following the legal end to segregation in the Brown v. Board of Education of Topeka decision in 1954, many churches throughout the American South defied denominational resolutions and continued to preach distortions of the gospel accommodating their ideology of racial segregation.

The histories of American Christianity during the civil rights era do not always hold Southern believers to account for their support of Jim Crow. Some recent studies, however, have cast

2. Sanders, *Ministry at the Margins*, 130–31.
3. Sanders, *Ministry at the Margins*, 131–33.

religious institutions as actively involved in maintaining this apartheid-like system.

Carolyn Renée DuPont, for instance, looks at the three largest denominations in the American South following World War II: the Southern Baptists, the Methodists, and the Presbyterians. She argues that far from being carried along by culture, church members actively supported the unjust system of segregation and white supremacy even as they decried personal racism. It was not therefore the blatantly vocal racists who enabled this culture as much as it was those who passively sat in the pews and seemingly harbored no racial prejudice.[4]

Dupont focuses upon white evangelicals in Mississippi who promoted a kind of spiritualized gospel, one emphasizing personal salvation, evangelism, and a relatively narrow band of accepted readings of Scripture:

> The racial hierarchy required a certain theological approach—
> the specific understandings of salvation, morality, and biblical
> interpretation that dominated in the Magnolia State. Thus
> white evangelicals' efforts to retain segregation included intense battles to preserve the orthodoxy of their kind of evangelical belief. Simultaneous with their efforts to thwart black
> equality, Mississippi's evangelicals argued vigorously with
> other whites about the meaning and implications of Christianity. . . . Conservative evangelicals recognized that white
> religious champions of black equality generally embraced an
> essentially different Gospel.[5]

The promotion of this problematic gospel, therefore, involved more than race theory. Genuine differences as to how the Bi-

---

4. Carolyn Renée Dupont, *Mississippi Praying: Southern White Evangelicals and the Civil Rights Movement, 1945–1975* (New York: NYU Press, 2013), 2, 8–12.
5. Dupont, *Mississippi Praying*, 8.

ble should be read, as well as how the faith should be practiced, complicated the racial divide. During this tumultuous era, churches kept on meeting, the Bible was read, pastors offered sermons in support of racial segregation, hymns were sung, and baptisms conducted, but white Christians seemed oblivious to the evils of racial schism and the gospel of white supremacy.

What is concerning today is that a similarly accommodationist gospel is promoted in many of the same communities, as perversions of the gospel are likely to target the vulnerable, particularly undocumented immigrants, Dreamers, and refugees fleeing other parts of the world. Fixated on saving souls and protecting traditional values, church leaders can't discern the nationalistic and xenophobic character of the message being promoted in their churches. It is *not* difficult, however, for diverse or traditionally marginalized people to detect the odorous character of this distorted message.

What attracts many white Christians to this distorted gospel is often the uncertainty related to America's changing demographics. Fear of difference seems to be a common link between those who opposed racial "amalgamation" and church folk today who fear "the browning of America." Political leaders who promote the idea of a return to America's former greatness appeal to the subliminal racial and ethnic anxieties harbored by white believers.

The adoption of an anti-immigrant rhetoric within churches has exposed not only a divide between older and younger whites, but also between white Christians and other nondominant Christian groups, including Hispanics and those of Asian descent. Though most believers support legal immigration, the adoption of an anti-immigrant stance within churches shows a willingness on the part of white believers to modify the gospel in order to fit a fringe ideology not native to the church. Daniel Cox, a cofounder of the Public Religion Research Institute, writes about the influence of Donald Trump's aggressive anti-immigration platform on the white evangelicals who supported his presidential election in 2016:

> No issue exemplifies Trump's influence among white evangelical Christians—and highlights the emerging generational divide—more than immigration. From the start, Trump has made opposition to immigration a central part of his political identity. And white evangelical Christians rallied around Trump in the 2016 election and were quick to embrace his hard-line immigration agenda. During the campaign, white evangelical Christians expressed support for preventing Syrian refugees from entering the U.S. and temporarily banning Muslims from coming to the country. After the election, they coalesced in support of building a wall along the southern border and blocking immigration from majority Muslim countries.[6]

Evangelical support for the above policies ignores how often the Bible promotes the care of society's most vulnerable, and it masks the fact that many who flee to the United States from Latin America claim a Christian heritage.

Mark DeYmaz and Oneya Fennell Okuwobi, two pastors devoted to promoting multicultural congregations, show that many conducting ministry in the church world support faulty convictions. Among these is the "homogenous unit principle," which seeks to inculturate the gospel in a way that does not require converts to accept racial or ethnic difference. Along with this error, DeYmaz and Okuwobi also point to the celebration of "numerical growth and attendance" over "community revitalization and transformation." Adding to these errant habits of the heart is a preference for purchasing new land and buildings

---

6. Daniel Cox, "Could Trump Drive Young White Evangelicals Away From the GOP?," *FiveThirtyEight* (blog), August 20, 2019, https://fivethirtyeight.com /features/could-trump-drive-young-white-evangelicals-away-from-the-gop/.

rather than "repurposing abandoned space in the community" and failing to empower minority leadership. Finally, DeYmaz and Okuwobi assert that "calling for unity and justice on social media from the otherwise segregated churches that we lead or attend" ultimately undermines the church's witness.[7] Such short-sightedness testifies to the fact that a gospel wrongly conceived stands behind much of how the church conducts its ministry.

Our tendency to bend and twist the gospel to meet popular societal values must constantly be guarded against. In allowing these cultural traits to shape the message we preach, we open ourselves to the brokenness of culture, including its hierarchies. It is easier to recognize a modified gospel from a distance. Sometimes this distance is measured in years, while at other times it may be measured by a cultural border or boundary.

Gary Parrett writes about how he came to recognize the extent to which the gospel he had grown accustomed to had been modified. After his marriage to his wife, Holly, a Christian of Korean heritage, he returned with her to the land of her birth. There the couple attended church together. While participating in this congregation, Gary began to discover that aspects of the faith being practiced in what was to him a foreign setting were merely trappings of Korean culture being passed off as Christianity by church leaders. Subsequently, he and his wife traveled to Japan. In this new setting, they gradually became aware of the same kind of cultural modifications to the faith. Awakened to the relationship between faith and culture, the couple returned to the United States.

Having seen, for the first time, expressions of the faith in other cultures, I began to see how the faith had taken root

7. Mark DeYmaz and Oneya Fennell Okuwobi, *Multiethnic Conversations: An Eight-Week Journey toward Unity in Your Church* (Indianapolis: Wesleyan Publishing House, 2016), 146–47.

in my own cultural context. My home church was made up of people who were white, suburban or rural Americans, and, almost uniformly, politically conservative. On most Sundays, my wife was one of only two or three non-whites present in a congregation of more than two hundred people. Many of the members were active politically in support of Republican candidates and causes. Members lived comfortably, many on large plots of land that ensured plenty of space and privacy. Church was run very democratically. . . . This is how things had always been in my church. But I now began to suspect that we had, as a community, assumed that God was one of us. He too was white, English-speaking, American, evangelical, and Republican. We had wrapped him up in the red, white, and blue and weekly served him up with a slice of mom's apple pie.[8]

Holly had trouble ministering in the congregation they chose to attend. Over time, she could see that people believed that whatever endeavor the United States found itself entangled in was justified. As a member of the intercessory prayer ministry team, she had the opportunity to help her sisters and brothers see beyond their limited cultural horizon. Such insight, however illuminating, wasn't always appreciated by all the members of the group. In fact, it was later suggested that perhaps Holly wasn't quite ready to serve on the prayer team.[9]

This scenario draws attention to the cost incurred when we don't embrace the diverse members of the body of Christ. Holly had been blessed with a perspective and insight not shared by many in her prayer team. She was a gift to that particular ministry, whether it was recognized or not. Holly helped the group remain committed to the idea that God was a God who loves

8. Elizabeth Conde-Frazier, S. Steve Kang, and Gary A. Parrett, *A Many Colored Kingdom: Multicultural Dynamics for Spiritual Formation* (Grand Rapids: Baker Academic, 2004), 45.

9. Frazier, Kang, and Parrett, *A Many Colored Kingdom*, 45.

the whole world, not a particular people or country. But faith too often becomes entangled with nationalistic tendencies. The ability to identify these counterfeit expressions of the faith is critical to working toward unity.

What adds fuel to such distortions of the gospel is often messaging from sources considered reliable allies in the promotion of a credible faith agenda. Among these are Christian news services and Christian radio programs. Together these offerings profess to advocate for traditional family values under the umbrella of an overarching conservative political agenda. These same programs are generally believed to be broadcasting under the imprimatur of the gospel. Along with the above resources, many Christians also draw heavily from conservative talk shows and cable news outlets tailoring the "news" to support and defend a partisan political ideology.

With a fairly long drive to reach the university where I taught for a decade, I had more time than most to tune in to the radio. In November of 2018, I was listening in to a particularly moving song with lyrics focused on the "reckless love of God." This popular Christian song expresses God's boundary-busting, wall-kicking-down pursuit of his children.

In stark contrast to the celebration of this gracious sentiment expressed in the song, however, was the news story that followed. The anchor detailed the arrival of a caravan of immigrants at the southern border of the United States. Borrowing from the inflammatory rhetoric of politicians, the news service quoted a local official's characterization of the arrival as an "invasion." These people were not viewed as vulnerable victims, fleeing their homes in search of a better life for their families; rather, they were enemies to repel.

Following the news, the listener was greeted by the morning show hosts. With apparently little thought for the way in which the aforementioned characterization of immigrants might play in the body of Christ, the perky morning hosts pivoted immediately to speak about the ongoing persecution of Christians in a former Eastern Bloc country. The hosts seemed to be completely unaware of the fact that an overwhelming number of those streaming to the US border at the time would have considered themselves Christian. Though concern was raised for Christians far away in a European country, no such concern was raised for the Christians suffering right at our border. A right-wing political agenda—based as it is on a problematic set of assumptions about ourselves, our institutions, our diverse sisters and brothers, and even about God—does not mix well with the gospel of Jesus. The blending of two very different streams of messaging, the universal love of God and the denigration of asylum seekers, leads to the creation of a perverted gospel, one widely disseminated throughout the American church.

Polarizing Rhetoric

Church folk have developed quite an appetite for such divisive and polarizing rhetoric as disseminated by cable news outlets and radio talk show hosts. Such a menu—filled out as it is by constant diatribes against the politics of individuals who support the social safety net, racial justice, and initiatives to promote secondary education and environmental conservation—has taken its toll. Believers who hold such opinions are not portrayed as sisters and brothers in the faith, but rather as misguided and dangerous to the country—enemies, even. The talking heads often make use of religious rhetoric in their support of divisive and hateful ideas. To be fair, damning rhetoric is also heard on left-leaning cable outlets, but that is not the kind of distortion that I face in the part of the country where my ministry is carried out.

Because of the lack of connection between white Christians and Christians of color, such diatribes go unchallenged or are passed off as reactions against political correctness. When objections are raised, the objectors are criticized as agitators. Nightly, the stars of cable media are welcomed into the homes of committed followers of Christ. These same church folk see no disconnect between the divisive rhetoric they consume from cable news and what they hear on the weekends in their respective houses of worship.

There is ample evidence showing that many Christians have inherited a siege mentality. The messaging broadcast by the media and echoed in our churches claims that we as believers are at war—with society, with the opposing political party, or with the wrong kind of Christians. A combative posture positions us well to fight the culture wars, but it does little to promote unity. Such problematic thinking must be reevaluated in light of Christ's prayer for oneness and the supporting New Testament teaching on the essential unity of Christ's church.

In the pursuit of unity, it may be necessary for Christians to monitor more carefully the kind of programming we choose to consume. As was indicated before, the more problematic stream of divisive religious propaganda I encounter comes from the right wing of the political spectrum. I find myself regularly attempting to offer an antidote to what is disseminated in our media. I work at trumpeting a perspective that is more grace filled, expansive, generous, and unifying. At the same time, I must really combat my own tendency to become negative and divisive in my role as a pastor.

Election season brings out the worst in Christians in terms of the practice of unity. More troubling is the idea that the ugliness that comes out in these election cycles simply remains in us perpetually, even if hidden most of the time. History tells us that Christians can be cruel and self-centered. Despite the Bible's message about caring for the vulnerable, believers can be remarkably ignorant of the pain and suffering of those living on the margins.

Can Religion Make Us Better People?

In my distress over the divisiveness I witnessed in the broader church throughout the 2012 election cycle, I was forced to consider the question of whether religion can make us better people. Though the answer might seem astoundingly obvious, at that particular moment I was decidedly less certain. Looking back over this period, my dismay was due in part to the promotion of a distorted gospel. The perversion of the message of Jesus allows individuals to live comfortably in a divided and unreconciled state.

In my experience as a church leader, it seems that too often religion does little to make us better people. By "better" I mean more loving, kind, compassionate, and selfless. Indeed it appears the Christian faith sometimes yields less than positive results for a person's character. The religion we embrace isn't always characterized with humanity's best impulses. In far too many instances it is possible to discern a disconnect between the gospel as related in the Bible, and a tainted, weaponized version of the "good news" too often presented to polarize American society.

In this difficult season in my ministry, I considered the campaign of Pope Urban II, who in the eleventh century called for the first of what would become multiple Crusades. Similarly, my thoughts went to the Salem witch trials and the mistreatment of America's indigenous inhabitants. And of course I could not ignore the bloody religious conflicts of the Reformation period.

With the election in full swing, with xenophobia and bigotry pervading the ranks of the faithful, it occurred to me Christian religion too often makes us certain of our rightness, more confident in putting others in their place, more proud of our spiritual achievements. I sometimes think our practice of religion can actually make us more unpleasant and difficult to be around.

History provides examples of individuals who have discerned how religion can corrupt people of faith. For example, one such individual was Hatuey, a sixteenth-century Taino leader who opposed the colonization of his people by the Spanish on what is today the island of Cuba. Faced with the exploitation of his people and the greed of the Spaniards, he is reported to have gathered a group of indigenous hearers and pointed to a basket of gold jewelry and claimed, "Here is the God of the Christians." He was subsequently condemned to death. When asked whether he might want to be baptized in order to escape the fires of hell, he is reported to have asked if Christians go to heaven. When his accusers said "yes," he related that he preferred hell.[10] The gospel promoted by the Spanish colonizers was, in the eyes of those like Hatuey, unappealing. We who have been entrusted with the gospel must also be aware of our one tendency to befoul the good news.

Championing a faith focused on actions of love goes far in keeping us from promoting a problematic version of the faith. Such a shift in emphasis places more importance on living out the directives of Scripture. Allen Yeh's diagnosis of what is errant with evangelical Christianity is likely more true of the faith as practiced in the United States than we care to admit. For Yeh, evangelical faith overemphasizes propositional truth but doesn't extend enough care and concern for at-risk populations, many of whom are majority Christian. Set against Western evangelicalism's emphasis on "intellectual assent," a focus on right living is needed. This does not mean relativism or the call for more effort is the best course of action. Yeh writes, "We need to stop resembling the Pharisees and focus more on the marginalized: on black and brown people who are dying, on refugees, on immigrants, on the poor. We need to act justly, love mercy, and walk humbly with our God."[11]

10. Bartolomé de Las Casas, *A Short Account of the Destruction of the Indies*, ed. and trans. Nigel Griffin (1542; repr., London: Penguin, 1992), 27–29. See also Ondina E. González and Justo L. González, *Christianity in Latin America: A History* (Cambridge: Cambridge University Press, 2008), 29.

11. Allen Yeh, "Theology and Orthopraxis in Global Evangelicalism," in *Still*

An intentional return to neighbor love does much to restore balance to the Christian faith. The way of life for the believer should be the "way of love," says Brian McLaren. Rather than thinking of the faith merely as an allegiance to a set of right beliefs, we should instead think of it as a commitment to living the way of love. This approach changes the way we think about church. When the way of love is our aim, then church becomes a place where we are trained to live with others in love. Such a curriculum would begin with love for one's neighbor. This same approach would, however, require growth and expansion. An emphasis on love for those near would be followed by an emerging love for one's enemies. We start with neighbor love (Love 101); we then are able to love self, then love the earth, and finally love God (Love 401).[12] A radical relationality becomes the center of such an approach. Nearness to God corresponds to one's way of relating to people. An emphasis on human relationships would certainly add credibility to the church's witness.

Barbara Brown Taylor seems to take up a similar starting point when discussing the story of the Good Samaritan (Luke 10:25–37):

> Jesus does not care what the Samaritan believes. It is only what the man does that matters. So he reads a different Scripture; so he goes to a different temple; so he follows a different path, so what? Jesus is focused on the man's actions, not his beliefs. This can be upsetting to Christians who have been taught that it is our faith and not our works that matter. But there you have it. Jesus was not a very good Protestant. He was a Jew who knew that right belief does not put a cup of water in the hands of a thirsty person or bandage a wound or offer

Evangelical? Insiders Reconsider Political, Social, and Theological Meaning, ed. Mark Labberton (Downers Grove, IL: InterVarsity Press, 2018), 104–18.

12. Brian McLaren, *The Great Spiritual Migration*, YouTube, September 28, 2016, https://www.youtube.com/watch?v=BHpQpgU-uPE.

a traveler a bed. Right beliefs don't change a thing unless they lead to right actions.[13]

In summary, believers must take care to promote the gospel of Jesus, a grace-filled message that takes seriously neighbor love. Far too often discordant voices driven by hateful ideologies pervert the message of our Lord who prayed that we would be one. The myriad of ways the gospel can be distorted by additions and subtractions must be avoided. Instead, the good news we preach should make us better people. It must inspire in us that same border-crossing, boundary-bursting love we find in the New Testament. To settle for less is to embrace a hollowed-out message, a false gospel. In the next chapter, we will focus on pragmatic steps to promote oneness.

UPPER ROOM EXERCISES

Reflection

Reflect on your own consumption of the divisive rhetoric coming from cable news, Facebook, and other sources. To what extent has this rhetoric impacted you?

Questions for Discussion

1. Discuss the United States' cultural influence on the faith you practice. Are there elements of the culture that might be inconsistent with the practice of Christianity? Explain.
2. What do you make of the church's witness during the civil

---

13. Barbara Brown Taylor, *The Right Answer*, YouTube, July 16, 2013, https://www.youtube.com/watch?v=wds3OxzHNAI.

rights era? Does the broader church today do a better job relating to Hispanic Christians? Explain.

3. Discuss an instance when you think the Bible was used to hurt another individual or group.

4. Reread the story of the good Samaritan. With which character do you most identify? How does this teaching story relate to the practice of unity?

From Pew to Practice

Since the political process appears at times to be injurious of the cause of unity in the church, take the time to read over the platform of the political party you support. What planks of this platform do you most appreciate? Which do you find more problematic? Do the same with the party you are least likely to support. Discuss your findings with a trusted friend or colleague.

Chapter Seven

From Pew to Practice

For people of privilege, reconciliation begins with sinking to our knees before God.

—*Sami DiPasquale*

Beginning to implement practices that promote oneness doesn't have to overly stress overworked church leaders and members. New programming or other taxing initiatives need not be the first step in the process of more faithfully living out Jesus's call for unity. Instead, the church might make use of its liturgical tradition, promotional materials, websites, artwork, worship resources, and scheduled church and community events to begin facilitating the practice of oneness. In this chapter, I will mention several of these before developing a few in more detail. It should be clearly stated that these steps are modest; they are first steps in making a good start. Those serious about the cause of unity must continue to put one foot in front of the other allowing themselves to journey ever onward, upward, and outward toward God and the diverse other.

A church or denominational group can make use of its unique theological heritage to bring to the fore the importance of the practice of unity. In the *Catechism of the Catholic Church*, for example, one discovers how the celebration of the Eucharist reveals the united character of the body of Christ. Living members gathered to receive the Lord's Supper are joined by believers who have passed to heaven. No distinction is made in rank based on nationality, ethnicity, race, age, or income status. The richness of this practiced conviction can be highlighted in various ways that might draw attention to its promotion of oneness.[1]

Sermons, homilies, and small-group lessons can take up appropriate Bible passages highlighting the promotion of unity. When the particular context out of which the passage has been selected is sufficiently developed, insight for today's church can be applied to instances of disunity plaguing God's people in the present era. Illustrations and examples employed in sermons and homilies offer an additional opportunity to promote inclusiveness and unity. I once attended a church gathering where several older congregants from area churches came together. This recurring meeting historically has included very little ethnic and racial diversity. On this occasion, the evangelist concluded the message with a video recording of a rousing spiritual sung by a black choir. The strategic use of this beautiful and moving recording illustrated for everyone assembled the breadth and diversity of the body of Christ.

In order to promote unity, prayers can be penned and readings offered. Musical selections can also be chosen to illustrate the universal scope of the body of Christ. Authors and musical artists chosen from diverse demographics may embody elements of the church not often heard from in mostly white worship settings. Offerings by Hispanic and Asian church leaders and artists remind congregants the body of Christ includes more than Christians gathering together in an otherwise insulated relational network.

Choices as to how a church facility will be decorated, the posters on the walls, the paintings that hang in the common

---

1. "The Sacrament of the Eucharist," *Catechism of the Catholic Church*, 1325, 1331, http://www.vatican.va/archive/ccc_css/archive/catechism/p2s2c1a3.htm.

fellowship area, can promote diversity and the practice of unity. I once visited a large congregation made up of senior members in a wealthy suburban area. The church was almost exclusively white. There wasn't much racial diversity in the community and noticeably less in the congregation. Yet one of the teen members took the initiative to paint a mural on the wall in the children's ministries section of the building. Three young people were depicted all standing together singing from a hymn book—a young woman and two young men, a Caucasian, and an African American. Without fanfare this teenage artist illustrated a segment of the diversity found in the body of Christ, a diversity yet to come to full fruit in his home fellowship.

Unity services, denominational gatherings, musical concerts, youth meetings, retreats, and community events provide opportunities for the practice of unity as well. These gatherings are often the first steps toward the practice of visible unity. In such assemblies, diverse groups are brought into close proximity. Real and meaningful exchange can occur in such settings. However, given the decline in denominational alignments, and the press of family schedules, church leaders must be strategic in their promotion of events beyond regularly scheduled worship services.

Chances are good that many religious bodies already produce publications and promotional material. These efforts can be harnessed to facilitate the practice of unity. For example, many denominational groups and congregations already publish newsletters and bulletins. More resourced congregations also maintain web pages as well as presences on other social media platforms. Unity can be promoted through strategic use of these same resources without much additional effort.

At the Beechwood Church of God, our small congregation in rural Ohio, a survey of how the newsletter promoted a spirit of oneness and unity across several fronts is illustrative. Though this was originally a print publication, we made it available to members online. In many settings the idea of a printed newsletter is obsolete. There are nonetheless many ideas presented below that will be translatable in this digital age. Obviously, security and privacy must be taken into consideration.

Beechwood Church of God's newsletter promoted unity for six years. The publication, issued from September through May, was titled *The Beechwood Christian Educator* (*BCE*), and each issue featured a different member of the congregation. Sometimes these biographical offerings focused on seniors in the congregation. In one issue a local farmer who had recently been diagnosed with cancer was introduced.[2] The publication also featured teens and youngsters. For example, a September 2008 entry spotlighted a young woman in the congregation who had finished second in the high jump at the state track meet. Another article drew attention to a preteen who began a project to benefit soldiers serving in Iraq.[3] Some of these articles highlighted former clergy and church members who attended the congregation in previous generations.

Sometimes articles detailed what was happening in sister churches aligned with the Church of God movement. One included a story about the restart of a congregation in a nearby community, providing the pastor's account of the successful launch and emphasizing the importance of prayer throughout the process.[4] Another issue featured a newly established congregation opening in a neighboring community. It detailed the challenges this new church plant would potentially encounter.[5] In service of unity beyond this local gathering, the newsletter made it possible for congregants to keep pace with what was going on in districtwide movement gatherings. Sometimes articles in the newsletter connected the congregation to Church

2. *Beechwood Christian Educator* (*BCE*), September 2006, 2.
3. *BCE*, May 2008, 2.
4. *BCE*, October 2006, 2.
5. *BCE*, September 2006, 2.

of God mission activities outside the United States. One article, for example, announced the selection of two local leaders picked to head up mission efforts in Tanzania.[6]

At the time of my arrival at the Beechwood congregation, it was largely made of members with no real connection to the pioneers who founded the church. Connecting the congregation to its history seemed important. The newsletter allowed congregants to learn about its past members—an aspect of the practice of unity that is, frankly, often overlooked. A series of articles detailed the history of the two congregations (Gratis and Beechwood) that had merged in 1983 to form what is now Beechwood Church of God. The names of the clergypersons who held leadership roles in the life of the congregation were highlighted in these articles as well.

In support of unity beyond the congregation, individuals from outside the church sometimes contributed to the newsletter. For example, Michelle Mosier, adjunct professor of theology at Xavier University in Cincinnati, was recruited to pen articles on the important role women in ministry were playing in our movement. As in many traditional congregations, women have not often been called on to fill vacant pastoral leadership roles. The newsletter offered a way to educate the congregation about the challenges being faced by women pursing the vocation of ministry. Mosier wrote about her family, education, and ministry. She also wrote about her mentoring of women serving as clergypersons. Revealing her passion for building unity, she offered the following:

> I am proactive for the inclusion of all people to participate fully in the life of the church regardless of age, race, ethnicity, gender and mental or physical capabilities. I have a heart to reach out to the poor and marginalized in society, loving those

6. *BCE*, September 2006, 2.

who are overlooked and often forgotten. I also do all that I can to find opportunities for women to lead and pastor within the church.[7]

The newsletter sometimes spotlighted diverse congregations and ministries. In one installment of the newsletter, an article detailed the establishment of the Eleventh Street Church of God, then located in Middletown, Ohio. This same offering listed the names of the pastors who led the church from its founding through its then current leader. The article also described the erection of the building where the congregation was then meeting. Because many attendees at the Beechwood Church did not have a strong connection to our movement, it is likely that most did not even know the small African American congregation existed, though it was located fewer than ten miles away.[8]

Beechwood Church resides in a homogenous community. The opportunity to introduce stories about the lives of people of color was an important editorial objective in support of the practice of unity. In one issue the life and work of Daniel Rudd, an African American, Jim Crow-era, Catholic civil rights leader was featured.[9] In another article, attention was drawn to Gloria A. Robison, a minister from South Carolina who had recently visited the church and shared her powerful story of racial violence and redemption:

> Sister Gloria Robinson visited our congregation in June of this year and shared her story. I have been telling anyone who will listen that I think she should be the "poster-saint" for our movement. She was born out of wedlock in Aiken, South Carolina. Gloria was raised by her grandparents. She grew up in a

7. *BCE*, March 2013, 1–2.

8. Herschel Caudill, *History of the Church of God in Middletown, Ohio, from 1909* (Middletown, Ohio, 1991), quoted in *BCE*, November 2009, 1.

9. *BCE*, December 2011, 1–2.

part of the state notorious for Klan activity. When the school bus passed, the children often spat out the window at them. If they heard a car coming down the road, she and [her] siblings hid out. Blacks didn't own cars. On one occasion Gloria's uncle made the mistake of identifying some Klan members, who in turn made a threat to get him. One night when her grandfather was working, the Klan set the house on fire. Her brother and two sisters perished in the blaze. Gloria was so badly burned she was in hospital for a couple of years. Against incredible odds she was able to realize her dream of becoming a nurse. She was subsequently ordained as a Church of God pastor. Without bitterness in her heart, she shares the love of Jesus with others. Her church is located on the property where the fire took the lives of her siblings.[10]

Other articles reveal a commitment to unity across denominational lines. One contribution detailed a remodeling project then in progress at a Methodist congregation in the community. Another piece reviewed Matthew A. Sutton's book on Foursquare Church founder Aimee Semple McPherson.[11]

Sometimes articles printed in the newsletter more directly highlighted historic examples of disunity within the church. For example, in a reprint of an 1898 article from the Church of God publication *The Gospel Trumpet*, the contributor spoke about the color line; he writes, "How can we have confidence in people's profession of sanctification when there are marks, manifestations, and feelings of prejudice, whether it be against Africans, Chinese, Spanish, Egyptians, Jews, or the poor of our own race? Salvation must and will bring God's people into fellowship and communion in the Holy Spirit, regardless of nationality."[12]

10. *BCE*, December 2013, 1.

11. *BCE*, December 2012, 1. Matthew A Sutton, *Aimee Semple McPherson and the Resurrection of Christian America* (Cambridge: Harvard University Press, 2009).

12. *Gospel Trumpet*, 12 December 1898, quoted in *BCE*, December 2013, 1.

In another offering I wrote:

> The world now more than ever needs to see the Church as a countercultural example of how people can live in authentic community unmolested by class. . . . On the other hand, the political system works by pitting one against another in order to maximize votes for one party or another. The spirit of division must be kept outside the church. We must not allow it to divide the members of Christ's Body. We are taught that in Christ there is no Jew or Gentile, no slave or freeman, no male or female. The divisive prejudices which attend these differences are null and void in Christ. We in the church are to demonstrate this unity by the way we conduct our lives.[13]

This sampling of articles meant to encourage unity across various fronts of division serves as an example of what might be done by churches seeking to take beginning steps toward the promotion of the practice of unity.

Cultural Coach and Mentor

Because of the need to cross boundaries and borders well, one more ambitious practice that might be employed for the serious practitioner of unity is to engage a mentor of color or a cultural informant. Such a practice should be done with great sensitivity. Not only could the learning be quite unsettling for the mentee, but the process might also be emotionally taxing on the mentor.

Nonetheless, the potential benefits of such a relationship, particularly for the mentee, are many. In these more structured cross-cultural exchanges, privileged groups (primarily white males) are afforded the opportunity to see the world from a per-

---

13. *BCE*, March 2013, 1.

spective of a nondominant member of society. Systemic racism, racially charged comments, barriers to progress, and the reality of privilege all can be unearthed as a result of this purposeful interaction and exchange. The mentor of color is able to share stories and give examples and illustrations that open up troubling vistas for the mentee.

In his book *A Brief Moment in the Son: Rediscovering the Gospel of Love and Reconciliation*, pastor Jay Harvey recounts his own experiences with a mentor of color and recommends the same to others open to reconciliation. Harvey suggests that this relationship be between twelve and eighteen months in duration. He further advises, "Do not let this relationship be a two-way mentorship. Sit and listen. Sit at the feet of your brother or sister and lean in and listen. Listen deeply and listen even harder when it becomes uncomfortable. Every time you get the urge to speak, don't."[14]

The time spent with his mentor changed Harvey. His ministry displays a developed concern for individuals who have been disadvantaged. His sensitivity to people at the margins, however, doesn't feel polluted by the type of inherent superiority too often characterized by Christian efforts to minister to the vulnerable. In his book, Harvey raises a series of questions revealing a more developed sense of our connectedness to people too often devalued by the church and society. Moreover, he recognizes their innate richness. He raises the following questions aimed at his readers: "Do you believe people on the margins of society who are believers have something to offer? Do you believe people on the margins of society who are believers have something you need?"[15]

Harvey elaborates: "Until believers come to the realization that other believers in their own communities with lesser means,

---

14. Jay T. Harvey, *A Brief Moment in the Son: Rediscovering the Gospel of Love and Reconciliation* (self-pub., 2019), 65.

15. Harvey, *A Brief Moment in the Son*, 62.

different views, and lesser status have something they need, then nothing will change. What is being sought in the way of growth, identity, and credibility in the contemporary church comes through reconciliation with others in the body of Christ."[16]

Harvey echoes a sentiment here that Cheryl Sanders relates. Individuals at the margins of society should not be viewed as *objects* of ministry, merely as those needing to be ministered to. Instead, she draws attention to the fact that we must recognize the agency of people at the margins who are engaged in the important work of ministry. To put it succinctly, ministry happens at the margins because those at the margins are doing ministry. Drawing attention to the outpouring of the Spirit on the day of Pentecost, Sanders reminds us that Peter understood this watershed event as a fulfillment of the prophecy found in the book of Joel. "Children and slaves, the ones most vulnerable, the ones most easily exploited and abused, the ones whose oppressed state is most readily discerned—these are the ones God has chosen to receive the outpouring of the Spirit and to bear the prophetic proclamation."[17]

Harvey's ideas for encouraging racial reconciliation also show evidence of a more broadly conceived perspective of ministry. His proposal for establishing multiracial congregations, something he refers to as the "Christian Exchange Program," identifies the locus of authority among willing African American church leaders. Those white Christians with a heart for the establishment of multiracial congregations are encouraged to sign a covenant to attend an inner-city church for a two-year period. They in turn are expected to tithe, volunteer, and journal their experiences. They are not, however, to take leadership roles in their new assignments. Harvey's sensitivities appear to be mov-

16. Harvey, *A Brief Moment in the Son*, 62.
17. Cheryl J. Sanders, *Ministry at the Margins: The Prophetic Mission of Women, Youth & the Poor* (Downers Grove, IL: InterVarsity Press, 1997), 75.

ing toward those of the community he seeks to engage, a sure sign of unity's influence.[18]

READING AS A PRACTICE OF UNITY

Reading as a devotional discipline is promoted in religious groups of all varieties, and it can be an important exercise in the promotion of unity. When what is being read uncovers and challenges problematic attitudes and biases, or introduces new perspectives and points of view, reading is a valuable practice of unity. This type of transformative reading allows individuals to understand others. It brings into clearer focus their experiences, stories, fears, and hopes. For the curious seeker, the practice lays open the collective insight and wisdom of a diverse group. It reveals dead-end paths as well as roads yielding more positive results. Reading the writings of diverse others can plant a seed that will blossom into something much more substantial. Reading is an initial step—understanding can increase, and before you know it you are seeing the world differently, more completely. This vision allows one to walk more closely to others.

Prior to my entrance into the university, I didn't read much material other than the Bible. It was in the academic setting I began to encounter diverse people and perspectives on issues I believed to have been settled. In this season of growth, I fell in love with reading. The practice markedly changed my way of seeing the world.

I still recall reading books that reshaped how I viewed myself, my country, and the diverse groups living around me, as well as a host of other issues. In those first few years at university, I began to recognize that others believed in God as I did; some were just as sincere and devoted as I was, and some were more committed

18. Harvey, *A Brief Moment in the Son*, 66–67.

to their faith. As I continued on this track, the religious figures I idolized in my youth had to take their place behind other visionaries about whom I was learning.

At university the baffling and beautiful complexity and diversity of the world pierced the insulated bubble I inhabited. Through reading I came to see that others experienced the world differently than I did. I began to appreciate literature, poetry, and the arts. I learned about other cultures and their histories, languages, and customs. I gleaned from the insight contained in other religious traditions. I began to see the genius of our nation's founding fathers set alongside their shortsightedness and discouraging pragmatism. I learned of the plight of the indigenous peoples of the Americas. I reveled in the writings of Benjamin Franklin even as I learned how our American political leaders were sometimes complicit in creating unjust systems. What I was learning was profitable but painful nonetheless.

In a history course the curriculum included a number of volumes that opened my eyes to the reality of war, suffering, violence, and injustice. We read Ron Kovic's *Born on the Fourth of July*, a story that related the violence of the war in Vietnam. We read Dee Brown's *Bury My Heart at Wounded Knee: An Indian History of the American West*, a work that opened my eyes to the displacement of indigenous populations through broken treaties and armed conflict. Another formative volume was Anne Moody's *Coming of Age in Mississippi: An Autobiography*. Her experiences growing up in poverty in the rural South had a disturbing impact. Finally, Upton Sinclair's *The Jungle* provided a glimpse into the challenges faced by immigrants in the nineteenth century. This same work complicated my understanding of the American capitalistic enterprise.[19]

19. Ron Kovic, *Born on the Fourth of July* (New York: McGraw-Hill, 1976); Dee Brown, *Bury My Heart at Wounded Knee: An Indian History of the American West* (New York: Holt, Rinehart & Winston, 1970); Anne Moody, *Coming of Age*

As a PhD student, I was afforded the opportunity to spend five years reading every issue of a black Catholic newspaper published from Cincinnati and Detroit by Catholic civil rights activist Daniel A. Rudd. Dating from 1886 to 1893, these issues reveal America from the perspective of a black entrepreneur and activist. His editorials chronicle what he witnessed both in society and in the church. I experienced in some small measure a bit of the frustration and disappointment Rudd felt as Jim Crow legislation began to be passed in states formerly part of the Confederacy.

These and other readings allowed me to catch a glimpse of the world from beyond where I stood. At about the same time, I penned a few lines describing how these books had impacted me.

> *Books and Boundaries*
> Standing before page and threshold trembling—
> Hungry and naïve in a world of wonder
> Still voice calling from a distance—
> Answered over mountains of the immediate
>   and present
> Your inky insides irresistible
> Fumbling fingers in typed treasures volumes thick—
>   Dickens, Vanauken, Hawthorne and Dostoevsky
> Worlds of wonder rushing in altering
>   inner landscapes
> New perspectives bent and borrowed
> Early rising, a few minutes more stealing—
> To bed late—my salty hands on you.
> In night's darkness holding you to the lamp—
> And you, me, to the light
> Longfellow's books were his shield and sword—
> You, my fast Clipper

Carrying me backwards and forwards to lands green
  and fertile
Bearing me from the shore of ignorance and error
Spying over your bow, the unspoiled land of growing
  and knowing

Reading with an Eye toward the Excluded

Having taught the history of Christianity for a number of years,
I see it as an important pedagogical task to illumine parts of the
Christian story often overlooked or ignored by students. Reading as a practice of unity must necessarily be directed toward
learning about diverse individuals whose contributions to the
development of Christianity have too often been missed. The
practice of unity is served well by finding these sources. A few
come readily to mind: Elizabeth Gillan Muir's *A Women's History
of the Christian Church*; Timothy Matovina's *Latino Catholicism*;
and *The History of Black Catholics in the United States* (1990) by
Fr. Cyprian Davis, OSB.[20] This list of recommendations could
be expanded by reviewing bibliographies found in similar books
and articles, or perhaps even through crowdsourcing.

There are so many more practices offering the potential to
promote unity in the body of Christ; a fitting list of some of
them is found in Sami DiPasquale's "Standing between Worlds"
in *Making Neighborhoods Whole*. Some have been covered; others
are equally worthy of implementation:

For people of privilege, reconciliation begins with sinking to
our knees before God. We can choose to build relationships

20. Elizabeth Gillan Muir, *A Women's History of the Christian Church: Two
Thousand Years of Female Leadership* (Toronto: University of Toronto Press, 2019);
Timothy Matovina, *Latino Catholicism: Transformation in America's Largest
Church* (Princeton, NJ: Princeton University Press, 2012); and Cyprian Davis,
The History of Black Catholics in the United States (New York: Crossroad, 1990).

with those outside traditional power structures, with people who are "other." We can listen to their stories, paying careful attention especially when we hear a pattern emerging. We can put ourselves under the authority of someone from a different cultural heritage. We can choose to live in a setting where we are the minority. We can study history and theology from the perspectives of those who were not invited into the process of creating the standard textbooks—history can sound so different based on who is telling the story. We can grieve the tragedies our forebears were a part of and try to figure out how they factor in to how we live today. We must ask God and others for forgiveness, and we must forgive ourselves. Finally, we must move forward, always listening, always striving to embrace voices from the outside with a resolve to confront the sin of injustice at every opportunity.[21]

In the final chapter, we will look at three individuals and one congregation committed to living out life in a posture of oneness. It is helpful to see how the practices and sensitivities detailed above become embodied in the lives of the faithful. Those highlighted set the pace for the rest of us who, frankly, have some catching up to do.

Upper Room Exercises

Reflection

A number of suggestions as to how your congregation might make use of current platforms, publications, and programs to promote the practice of unity have been offered in this chapter.

---

21. Sami DiPasquale, "Standing between Worlds," in *Making Neighborhoods Whole: A Handbook for Christian Community Development* (Downers Grove, IL: InterVarsity Press, 2013), 73–74.

Reflect on your commitment to getting involved. Do you see the work as meaningful?

Questions for Discussion

1. The practice of reading offers real potential for someone seeking to learn to practice unity. Are there books and articles you have read that you think would be good additions to the titles offered above?

2. What kinds of questions would you have for a cultural mentor or coach? What issues do you think they would raise in such a conversation? If you were to choose today, who would you ask to fill this important role?

3. Which practical suggestion above would be easiest for your church to implement as it gets intentional about the promotion of unity?

From Pew to Practice

Gather some like-minded folks from your congregation and look over the list of suggestions above. Either choose a couple of them or come up with your own list. Then with a heart full of love begin to intentionally practice unity.

Chapter Eight

Champions for a Cause

I love the people that I minister with. I don't want to not be able to engage. . . . I just see people in a lot of pain. . . . We all need to be held tight through a lot of stuff. What choice do we have, but unity, or walking together? I need people who think differently than I do. I need them! If I want to have a relationship with people who think differently than I do, then I have to work. . . . I like people. . . . Some people offend me while sitting there, but I still delight in their company. I can see why they are loved and beloved. What do you do?

—*Isabel Fernandez*

While teaching classes on diversity and inclusion throughout the country, I routinely use a simple instrument designed to encourage self-reflection on how well participants think they value and include those who might be viewed as different. In this setting we make use of a diagram outlining a spectrum of four stages. Stage one at the lowest end is characterized by intolerance and unconscious incompetence, and stage four at the other end signifies inclusion and unconscious competence.[1]

---

1. This method I borrowed from Eric M. Ellis, a diversity consultant who has made a marked impact on how I see the work of unity.

Because it is helpful to learn from individuals who embody practices promoting unity and respectful cross-border relationships, I often ask participants to identify someone from their network of acquaintances who is inclusive and engages diversity well. These border-crossers must have internalized the habits of heart and mind that make them ready exemplars. They must be free of the need to psyche themselves up for diversity; rather, diversity must be something they engage without really thinking. Knowing someone who fosters unity well helps those who want to learn by allowing them to observe a model of intercultural competency. To help the reader imagine how the practice of unity can be translated into our lives and our churches, this chapter highlights three individuals and one congregation.

Meeting Ann

In my work promoting inclusion and team building, a gifted woman (whom I will call "Ann") stands out. She embodies many of the habits and practices that make her a good role model. In a recent interview she offered the following: "To me [unity] is just who I am; it is what I do. Unity is just how I roll. I think for some people it is a constant thing they are always trying to do, trying to incorporate in their lives. But for me, unity is just who I am. It is something that I have always embraced; I seek it out. If you don't have it you are not living a full rich life. . . . I feel you are stagnant."[2]

With respect to her deftness at crossing borders, Ann no doubt benefited from her upbringing in a diverse home. This type of varied context seems to set people up to develop competencies that might otherwise be left dormant had they been socialized in homogeneous settings. For Ann, it is normal to

2. Phone interview by Gary B. Agee, Middletown, Ohio, September 24, 2019.

negotiate difference in constructive ways. She seems to practice unity without really thinking about it; it is second nature.

Ann is an African American woman, but she was raised by white adoptive parents. She describes her siblings as biracial. One sister, she explains, looks as if she could be Hispanic. She also has a brother with an intellectual disability. Not long before I interviewed her, she had taken him to a football game. His unusual behavior and acting out caught the eye of some of those seated near her, but to Ann these outbursts were hardly noticeable. She has also had to navigate controversial issues concerning gender and sexual orientation. Ann has a transgender niece who is gay. Coming of age in such a context seems to have given her a leg up as she daily—and comfortably—negotiates difference.

White Christians often attend racially homogenous congregations. Many of them also reside in neighborhoods bereft of the kinds of diversity described above. For this reason, they often lack the skills and sensitivities needed to effectively engage difference in a way that promotes unity. Even more worrisome is the fact that some who live in these communities think they negotiate dissimilarity better than they actually do. The way in which diversity is presented by these well-meaning people, as well as the language they use, can be off-putting and hurtful to diverse people. Because of their status, however, many well-positioned folks can get along fairly well without engaging difference.

The impact of insulation and isolation within homogenous communities is not without ill effect. Drawing on insights from social psychology, Christena Cleveland identifies the downside of what is termed "group polarization":

> These days, Christians can easily go their entire lives without spending time with those who are different from them. Unfortunately, the more we spend time with people who are essentially identical to us, the more we become convinced that our way of relating to both Jesus and the world is *the* cor-

rect way. Over time, our convictions grow stronger and our attitudes toward different ideas and cultural expressions of worship become more negative.[3]

In such a setting, Christians are socialized or "discipled" in a culture of division. They are fed a flavored gospel that accords with their understanding of the world and how it works. The blinders blocking their vision remain intact. Those at the margins, though related, become strangers. When these dwellers at the margins speak of God, the world, or the *missio Dei*, their words become more incomprehensible to those lacking a relationship with the diverse other.

When one's faith community encourages unity across boundaries and cultures, it reinforces the benefits of this important practice. Ann's Catholic faith has been instrumental in her embrace of diversity on the road toward unity. She describes a time during her youth that helped to shape her thinking about oneness:

> As you know I was raised Catholic. There was this church camp we used to go to, and we went a week to two weeks every summer. When we would go, there were whites, Hispanics, there were Filipinos and Haitians. . . . From the moment I was born to the time I left for college, I would go to this church camp. We would sit around every night after dinner; we would all go to the campfire, and we would sing songs by Harry Chapin. One of my favorite songs was "All my Life is a Circle." To me that song represented unity. We were all together; we would all eat together. We were all one. That was something that was rooted in our faith, in what we believed, that we were all in this together. There was no separation of class, religion, or color."[4]

3. Christena Cleveland, *Disunity in Christ: Uncovering the Hidden Forces That Keep Us Apart* (Downers Grove, IL: InterVarsity Press, 2013), 27.

4. Phone interview by Gary B. Agee, Middletown, Ohio, September 24, 2019.

Ann serves as an example for us to follow. Her faith is integrated into her practice of oneness across borders of difference. She benefited from being raised in a diverse setting, but many would-be practitioners of unity will have to seek out these types of diverse settings.

Isabel Fernandez

Another individual who models the practice of unity in an exemplary fashion is Isabel Fernandez. She currently serves as the director of mission effectiveness for Catholic schools in a diocese in Florida. Prior to moving into this position, she worked as a community organizer, and she has also served in a number of parish school settings. Isabel described how each of these positions require a developed ability to negotiate differences. Moreover, these jobs tasked her with helping those she served get better at negotiating differences; organizational effectiveness was at stake.

Isabel Fernandez currently oversees the ministry of forty-one schools in nine counties in central Florida. "Every kind of Catholic that can be imagined" resides in this region, she explains. There are Vietnamese communities, migrant communities, Mexican Catholics, Catholics from various Caribbean Islands, Puerto Ricans, and Filipinos, as well as Anglos. White Catholics living across this area are very diverse as well, Fernandez points out. Some she serves live in rural areas, others in the suburbs; many also reside in various urban centers throughout that part of the state. This diocese includes very wealthy Catholics, as well as communities relying on state assistance to help pay for their children's parochial education. In one "dual-language" school, the student body represents fifty different countries of origin. In an area of this size, Fernandez explains, there are differences on social issues, including opinions about women serving in ministry roles, the issue of marriage equality, and gun rights.

My orientation has to be one in which I can engage all the "tribes," ideologically, religiously. I find myself having to be able to talk and hear from very different types of people. In order to do that, you can't just be blank; that doesn't work. People do not like to talk to a blank slate, it turns out. . . . They know that everybody has a perspective, an opinion, or a location from which they come. You have to learn to share how you think and feel without also alienating people. And if you can share in a way that invites people to be themselves, then you can start to have more positive [engagement].[5]

In her comments Fernandez explains that in a ministry setting achieving "mere tolerance," as it is understood in some civic spaces, is not the ultimate goal. "I just find that unhelpful in ministry. . . . Because if I am shooting for tolerance, that is a really low bar."

She goes on to explain:

I love the people that I minister with. I don't want to not be able to engage. . . . I just see people in a lot of pain. . . . We all need to be held tight through a lot of stuff. What choice do we have, but unity, or walking together? I need people who think differently than I do. I need them! If I want to have a relationship with people who think differently than I do, then I have to work. . . . Some people offend me while sitting there, but I still delight in their company. I can see why they are loved and beloved. What do you do? . . . The opposite of unity is hardness of heart. When you walk with people, you get to know people. . . . You have to listen to them.

Part of this ability to practice unity, according to Fernandez, is expressed in a willingness to get behind their rhetoric, to see

5. Isabel Fernandez, phone interview by Gary B. Agee, Middletown, Ohio, October 4, 2019. All subsequent quotations from Fernandez are from this interview.

what is really going on. Individuals can be bigoted, but that is not necessarily the whole story.

> I had a guy tell me how much he couldn't stand the Hispanic people who moved into the house next door. The whole time I am thinking, "I am Hispanic. Do you know this?" I can take this as, he is trying to put me down, or that he is trying to thumb his nose at those people by doing it to me, knowing that I have to be polite to him because the church sent me. I could have interpreted that as a big power game. [But] I just saw someone who thought, "You are one of them, and I can talk to you." His great pain is that he cannot communicate with his neighbor. He really didn't mind that they were Hispanic. He minded because he couldn't talk to them. . . . Some people are full of hatred. That is for sure. I have seen that too, believe me. But there is a lot of frustration, isolation, and humiliation that gets interpreted as [hatred and bigotry]. . . . When you can get people past whatever the thing is that they have between them and just get them talking, they come to the [realization], "you are like me, even though you are nothing like me."

Drawing on the work of Roberto Goizueta, Fernandez points to an alternative for tolerance:

> The alternative is accompaniment. . . . It is the only way to get through "borderlands." I have found that ministry always happens at these crossroads—at these edges. . . . If you are going to be able to navigate that kind of territory where it is all contested. . . . You have to be able to be who you are, because people won't trust you otherwise. But at the same time, you have to be able to do it in a way that is inviting, open and willing to be corrected, informed, or connected. I find that I have to be vulnerable in certain kinds of ways that are appropriate . . . to be open to people, so they feel comfortable sharing of themselves.

For Fernandez there are various ways that one might describe the charism labeled as unity. At one time she really liked the idea of hospitality. Where this term comes up short for her, however, is that it fails to acknowledge that all of us are "guests." She adds, "None of the space is mine to welcome people into; we are all in borrowed space." Again, accompaniment best describes for her what it means to engage, to be really present for another who might be different across a number of fronts.

Fernandez exudes the kind of sensitivity, compassion, and desire to serve that are requisite for one who desires to practice unity. She also displays a developed set of border-crossing skills. Without thinking about it, she negotiates difference in a manner we would all do well to emulate.

Shannon New-Spangler

Sometimes the practice of unity can be costly to the individual who chooses to pursue it. Shannon New-Spangler, a minister who served for several years as a lead pastor in a church in the Midwest, suffered for the cause of oneness. This adversity flared up in part as a reaction to her principled attempts to bridge the racial divide between her congregation and the black churches in her community. These efforts brought opposition from the leadership in New-Spangler's charge. She later felt compelled to resign from her position.

For one seeking to live as a Jesus follower, New-Spangler believes unity is foundational. She says she harbors a growing awareness of God's plan to bring it to fruition. "We are meant to be connected; I feel like God created us to be connected." In looking back over her life and ministry, New-Spangler explains:

> One of the gifts God has given to me is empathy. Over the course of my childhood, into my teens, and on into my college years, I was aware of a racial division in society and the church,

but it was a slow awareness that grew into concern, and then motivation. . . .

Empathy is both tremendously painful and amazingly useful in the ministry setting. Although I would never claim to "know what it feels like," I began to embrace and accept the hurt I heard from brothers and sisters of color. After college it became abundantly apparent that I could no longer be an inactive advocate. . . . This knowledge has only intensified over the years. I firmly believe what Martin Luther King, Jr. said, "Our lives begin to end the day we become silent about things that matter." I have let myself continue to feel the rift that divisions cause in order to remind myself of the urgency of the quest towards unity. Unity must be pursued. For me it is not an option. I believe it to be part and parcel of living for God, living like Christ, and being filled with the Holy Spirit. Unity is essential and necessary to actually be the Body of Christ. It is foundational for the person who believes that we are all created in the image of God. The work of unity is a non-negotiable for me and for my ministry. [6]

With regard to New-Spangler's growing commitment to racial unity she writes:

A commitment to racial unity is something that has been developing my whole life. My parents always helped us to be aware of this issue. . . . But as a middle-class Christian and white person, until I entered ministry, I couldn't see that I needed to change. . . . That knowledge dialed up as I became more aware of the world and how churches function. . . . I just couldn't know about it; I needed to do something about it. . . . I needed to be actively in pursuit of unity.

6. Shannon New-Spangler, emailed interview response, October 10, 2019. Subsequent quotations from New-Spangler are from this interview response.

New-Spangler's commitment to racial reconciliation was indeed costly. About four years into her ministry placement, she began to promote racial unity more purposefully. As part of this ministry emphasis, she forged relationships with two African American congregations located near her. Joint worship services were held and sometimes were hosted by African American churches. Members of her church did not participate at the level she had hoped, however.

As New-Spangler began to make more significant efforts to bridge the racial divide between churches in her area, she found that her effectiveness in ministry eroded while opposition to her leadership began to mount. She writes, "My biggest challenge was in serving a congregation where many people, and much of the leadership, were resistant to the work. These conflicts eventually led to an understanding that my ministry and call did not match theirs." Her participation in events encouraging diversity and reconciliation were not welcomed, and she was urged to let it go. She finally left that congregation. New-Spangler's story reveals the very real cost of pursuing oneness. In it we recognize that courage is a necessary ingredient in the life of one who seeks to practice unity.

GARFIELD MEMORIAL CHURCH

In a season marred by polarization across society, Garfield Memorial Church, headquartered in a suburb of Cleveland, Ohio, stands out. The church gathers weekly at three different sites. The first is located in the relatively wealthy Pepper Pike neighborhood, a Jewish community. The second meeting site is in the community of South Euclid, nearer to the city of Cleveland. A third weekly gathering meets overseas in the African country of Liberia. The church is led by interracial couple Chip and Terri Freed, along with a talented and diverse group of staff members. Together this fellowship exudes a strong sense of purpose. The stated mission is to "make disciples of all people groups." The emphasis on gathering "all people groups" is not lost on anyone paying attention. Their vision for "widening the circle" has attracted people from various racial, ethnic, economic, and theological backgrounds. Congregation members, cheered on by their leaders, intentionally celebrate their church's growing diversity.

The promotional material prominently displayed in a space designed for fellowship expands upon the church's vision. "Our vision picks up the image of our church facility sitting upon a historic traffic circle here in Pepper Pike. The history of this church involved moving the facility out of the way so this circle and the traffic of people which it brought could occur. We want to continue in that tradition of widening the circle so that more and more people can experience the love of Jesus Christ."[7]

By the time Pastor Chip and his ministry partner Terri arrived at Garfield, the congregation was in decline, and the future of the church was in jeopardy, so they led the effort to embrace a cultural shift. The congregation made a number of important moves: It renewed its commitment to the Great Commission, determined to become outwardly focused, and embraced a vision of becoming economically diverse and multiethnic. The leadership team developed a new statement of purpose and began to promote a spirit of inclusion in worship. Finally, a diligent effort was made to recruit a diverse leadership team.[8]

During a recent staff meeting, Curt Bissel, the online campus pastor, initiated a program to solicit stories from the staff and leaders to illustrate and celebrate the congregation's diversity. "At Garfield diversity is more than a buzzword or even a nice value. It is at the heart of our core DNA," he said.[9]

7. "Mission, Vision, Values," Garfield Memorial Church, Pepper Pike, Ohio.

8. Mark DeYmaz and Bob Whitesel, *Re:Mix: Transitioning Your Church to Living Color* (Nashville: Abingdon, 2016), 42–44.

9. Gary B. Agee, personal notes collected during the Garfield Memorial Church staff meeting, October 2, 2019.

Garfield's leadership staff is diverse across a number of fronts. According to Terri Freed, who serves as the minister of reception, hospitality, and member care, this commitment to diverse leadership is intentional. In attendance at a staff meeting I visited were four African American leaders, including the congregation's teaching pastor, five women of various ages, and six men. Some were part-time, others full-time. The church selected these staff members not merely to fill a need, but rather to take on a role commensurate with each person's gifting.[10]

The agenda for the meeting was set not by Pastor Freed but rather by his able executive pastor, Terry McHugh. At this staff meeting, leaders took turns sharing what was going on in their respective areas of ministry. Pastor Freed allows staff members considerable latitude in carrying out their particular callings, and the appearance of a top-down hierarchal structure is purposely avoided.

Another rather remarkable aspect of Garfield's ministry is the fact that, though affiliated with Methodism, the staff is drawn from a variety of theological backgrounds, from Pentecostal to Mennonite. This diversity of theological heritage seems to be of no real concern for senior leadership. Among the ministries reported at the staff gathering I attended were small-group facilitation, acts of kindness, children's ministry, and a planned forum on racial issues that was to include high school students and local police officers.[11]

When Chip and Terri were called to the congregation, they were greeted by a congregation of roughly two hundred worshipers. Only seven African Americans attended the culturally white congregation. Pastor Freed explains: "I knew that the culture change had to happen. . . . Multiethnic ministry is a product of healthy evangelism. Too many of our churches are inward fo-

10. Agee, Garfield Memorial staff meeting notes.
11. Agee, Garfield Memorial staff meeting notes.

cused. So we had to break that [paradigm] and get them think-ing more outward. That was the big battle to begin."

Executive Pastor Terry McHugh explains that Pastor Freed really talked about the character of the diverse congregation he envisioned before it came to fruition. Having said this, it took about five years to change the culture. Part of this process was to help the congregation take on the mindset that the "most important" person attending church on any given Sunday was the "person who doesn't know Christ."[12]

> Changes were made to welcome individuals into the congrega-tion. Some of these changes involved making the church more inviting to the broader community. For example, images depict-ing an Anglo Christ were taken down. A commitment very early on was made to empower diverse leadership. Then the congrega-tion began to consider its identity. Initially, the goal was not to break down racism in the church, but rather to get us outward focused. In reaching out we began to engage diverse people.[13]

The congregation was encouraged to see itself more expansively as a "Cleveland church," rather than thinking of itself merely as a "Christian enclave" in a Jewish neighborhood. Such a reorientation broadened its members' field of ministry. This decision placed the congregation in a position where it could engage diversity along several fronts. As attendance began to increase, the church initi-ated a major renovation program to create a fellowship space more conducive to allowing congregants to get to know one another.

It isn't easy to practice unity, Pastor Freed explains. Two mes-sages he regularly communicates to his congregation include: "To be part of the church you have to be comfortable being un-

12. Chip Freed and Terry McHugh, interview conducted at Garfield Memo-rial Church, Pepper Pike, Ohio, October 2, 2019.
13. Freed and McHugh interview.

comfortable," and "You are going to like 70 percent of what happens here." He then goes on to explain to his members, "When you are in your 30 percent, someone else is in their 70 percent." "If you don't want to come to the family table because there is meatloaf on Monday, there is going to be pizza on Wednesday. But honor the family first."[14]

Terry McHugh puts it this way:

It is not about you, or your personal preferences. It is not that we don't care. We want to reach people in their musical and cultural language and honor that, but at the same time, we are always thinking about the people who are not here yet. . . . We want to be a church reflecting Revelation 7:9, a place where "people of every tongue, tribe, and nation worship together as one." That work to me has obviously never been more important than in our current cultural and political climate. . . .

Folks come in, and it is so stunning. There are people of every color in the rainbow. They are kind of like, "Wow, if they do that, there is probably room for me." In attendance we will have same-sex couples; we will have conservative evangelicals that think that same-sex marriage is totally wrong. And they will sit together on these couches having coffee. Isn't that what the church is supposed to be? If we can't have these conversations here, where are we going to have them?[15]

Pastor Freed admits that the unity the congregation enjoys came under threat in previous election cycles. He describes the 2016 election as "absolute hell." At one point in the election season when the racial rhetoric and hate speech reached a fevered pitch, he recalls preaching on unity from Ephesians 2. In this timely message, Pastor Freed emphasized the importance of grounding Garfield's unique unity-building work in the Bible. In the sermon,

14. Freed and McHugh interview.
15. Freed and McHugh interview.

however, he spoke directly to his members of color. He acknowledged that it might be tempting for them to drift back into a congregation where they bash Trump every Sunday. Conversely, he told his white members that he recognized the desire some might feel to find a church where they never had to hear "Black Lives Matter" and where they "prayed for the police every Sunday." He reminded the whole fellowship, "You guys are all here because you are committed to walking, working, and worshiping together as one, and reflecting church on earth as it is in heaven."[16]

As stated before, the temptation to settle for a cheap reconciliation or false unity is strong. Getting at the forces that push groups and individuals apart is not work for the faint of heart. The biases and prejudices that we carry with us are not easily exorcised. First, they hide out wherever they can find a dark corner of our being. Bringing them to light and working to evict them often means betraying the values and ideas of those with whom we have labored—individuals we love and cherish. In these moments we must choose to stand alongside our hospitable Lord; we must choose to walk in the light, to follow Christ.

This congregation and the exemplars highlighted above are standard-bearers for those willing to take on the task of answering Jesus's prayer for oneness. Unity in the body of Christ offers the world the most convincing proof that the gospel we share is indeed worthy of embrace.

UPPER ROOM EXERCISES

Reflection

Three individuals were highlighted above as exemplars with regards to the practice of unity. If someone were to write about your record regarding the negotiation of diversity, what might

16. Freed and McHugh interview.

they say? How does Garfield Memorial Church compare to the congregation or parish you attend? Does the mission of your church resemble that of Garfield's fellowship?

Questions for Discussion

1. How do you think Ann's early experiences with diversity in her home aided her in the practice of unity? Do you think parents and caregivers have an obligation to create opportunities in which youth and children are exposed to a broad range of diversity? Explain.

2. Reflect on the meaning of discipleship. If a church's homogeneity is a factor in making it more difficult to mentor Christians who cross boundaries and borders well, what might be done to produce believers committed to the practice of oneness?

3. Read over Isabel Fernandez's comments on unity. Offer a few Bible passages in support of such an approach to oneness.

4. Shannon New-Spangler felt as though she had to resign from her congregation when support for her efforts on behalf of racial reconciliation began to erode. Do you know anyone who has suffered for the cause of the practice of unity?

From Pew to Practice

Go on a quest to find a community leader with a reputation for positively engaging diversity. Schedule an interview. Among other questions, you might ask about their upbringing, their motivations, and the skills and sensitivities they employ in their practice of oneness. Get advice as to how you might improve your own practice of unity.

Finding Home

In this stream of oneness abundant life flows outward—toward the barren lands of fear, distrust, division, and discord.

God's unifying love is what animates a just and equitable fellowship or community. It is the life force that binds together the Godhead, spilling out onto the faithful who then together burst forth into harmonious song. In this stream of oneness, abundant life flows outward—toward the barren lands of fear, distrust, division, and discord. This life flow seeks to restore these wastelands to their fruitful end, making of them a home for us all.

I was once asked to accompany two dear saints on a visit to a gentleman with an intellectual disability. I will call him "Tommy." He lived in a group home in a community some four hours away from us, and his mother and grandmother were longtime members of our congregation. Because neither felt comfortable making the long drive, I went along as a chauffeur on a trip to celebrate his birthday. Moreover, I wanted to get to know Tommy because we had often prayed for him in our church gatherings.

Upon arrival at our destination, the joy of meeting Tommy washed over me. He received me warmly, like a brother. As it turned out, my responsibility in this festive event was to grill the hot dogs. I took my task seriously. We celebrated for a couple of hours, making the most of the time we had together. As the sun began to inch down in the sky, we prepared to say our goodbyes. I just knew that there would be a prayer offered before we departed; I knew just as certainly that I would be called to give that prayer.

As we gathered our things to make our departure, however, Tommy told his mother that he would be offering the prayer and that he would be doing so on my behalf. When the time came, Tommy came close, his sincerity warming the circle of petitioners. As I recall, he laid his hands on me. He shared his heartfelt conviction; he prayed for me, my family, and my ministry, though I'm not sure he knew how much I needed it. His was a genuine prayer of blessing, and I knew God was in it. Honestly, I may have learned more about the kingdom of God in that exchange than in all my years studying the finer points of theology.

As I prepared for services the following weekend, I couldn't stop thinking about that parting prayer and the upside-down (or perhaps right-side-up) nature of the community of the faithful. The kingdom of God is a fellowship where titles, degrees, human honors, and all our dismissive and diminishing labels lose their hold. Rather, it is one where we are bound together in love and oneness, each in God, dependent on the other. As I thought about Tommy's prayer, I saw myself as Abraham on a journey, I had traveled far to visit one to whom I thought I would minister. I carried my ordination, a history of completed theological degrees, and publications under my belt. I found, however, that in my encounter with Tommy, this "Abraham" met his "Melchizedek" (Genesis 14:18–20). And as the Scripture says, the "lesser was blessed by the greater" (Hebrews 7:7). In discovering this liberating insight, I felt like I had found my home.

Selected Bibliography

Burrow, Rufus, Jr. *Making Good the Claim: Holiness and Visible Unity in the Church of God Reformation Movement.* Eugene, OR: Wipf and Stock, 2016.

Caudill, Herschel. *History of the Church of God in Middletown, Ohio, from 1909.* Middletown, Ohio, 1991.

Cleveland, Christena. *Disunity in Christ: Uncovering the Hidden Forces That Keep Us Apart.* Downers Grove, IL: InterVarsity Press, 2013.

Committee on Cultural Diversity in the Church, United States Conference of Catholic Bishops. *Building Intercultural Competence for Ministers.* Washington, DC: United States Conference of Catholic Bishops, 2012.

Conde-Frazier, Elizabeth, S. Steve Kang, and Gary A. Parrett. *A Many Colored Kingdom: Multicultural Dynamics for Spiritual Formation.* Grand Rapids: Baker Academic, 2004.

Cosca, Rachel. "Just Unity: Toward a True Community of Women and Men in the Church." *Ecumenical Review* 66, no. 1 (March 2014): 39–52.

Daly, Jim. "The Importance of Listening in Today's Evangelicalism." In *Still Evangelical? Insiders Reconsider Political, Social, and Theological Meaning,* edited by Mark Labberton, 173–83. Downers Grove, IL: InterVarsity Press, 2018.

De Las Casas, Bartolomé. *A Short Account of the Destruction of the Indies.* First published in 1542. Edited and translated by Nigel Griffin. London: Penguin Group. 1992.

DeYmaz, Mark, and Oneya Fennell Okuwobi. *Multiethnic Conversations: An Eight-Week Journey toward Unity in Your Church.* Indianapolis: Wesleyan Publishing House, 2016.

DeYmaz, Mark, and Bob Whitesel. *Re:Mix: Transitioning Your Church to Living Color.* Nashville: Abingdon, 2016.

DeYoung, Curtiss Paul. *Coming Together in the 21st Century: The Bible's Message in an Age of Diversity.* Valley Forge, PA: Judson Press, 2009.

———. *Reconciliation: Our Greatest Challenge—Our Only Hope.* Valley Forge, PA: Judson Press, 1997.

DiAngelo, Robin. *White Fragility: Why It Is So Hard for White People to Talk about Racism.* Boston: Beacon, 2018.

DiPasquale, Sami. "Standing between Worlds." In *Making Neighborhoods Whole: A Handbook for Christian Community Development,* 68–74. Downers Grove, IL: InterVarsity Press, 2013.

Dupont, Carolyn Renée. *Mississippi Praying: Southern White Evangelicals and the Civil Rights Movement, 1945–1976.* New York: NYU Press, 2013.

Ellis, Eric M. *Diversity Conversations: Finding Common Ground.* 3rd ed. Cincinnati: Integrity Development, 2019.

González, Ondina E., and Justo L. González. *Christianity in Latin America: A History.* Cambridge: Cambridge University Press, 2008.

Harvey, Jay T. *A Brief Moment in the Son: Rediscovering the Gospel of Love and Reconciliation.* Self-published, 2019.

Helsel, Carolyn B. *Anxious to Talk about It: Helping White Christians Talk Faithfully about Racism.* St. Louis: Chalice Press, 2017.

Hill, Daniel. *White Awake: An Honest Look at What It Means to Be White.* Downers Grove, IL: InterVarsity Press, 2017.

Hines, Samuel George, and Curtiss Paul DeYoung. *Beyond Rhetoric: Reconciliation as a Way of Life.* Valley Forge, PA: Judson Press, 2000.

Johnson, Luke Timothy. *Sacra Pagina: The Gospel of Luke.* Vol. 3. Collegeville, MN: Liturgical Press, 1991.

———. *Sacra Pagina: The Acts of the Apostles.* Vol. 5. Collegeville, MN: Liturgical Press, 1992.

Locke, Attica. "In 'Heaven My Home' Attica Locke Shows a Part of Texas We Don't Usually See." Interview by Sam Briger. *Fresh Air*, October 16, 2019. https://www.npr.org/2019/10/16/770613459/in -heaven-my-home-attica-locke-shows-a-part-of-texas-we-don -t-usually-see.

Marshall, I. Howard. *Acts.* Tyndale New Testament Commentaries. Vol. 5. Leicester, England: Inter-Varsity Press, 1980.

Massey, James Earl. "Culturally Conscious Evangelism." In *Views from the Mountain: Select Writings of James Earl Massey*, edited by Barry Callen and Curtiss DeYoung, 215–24. Marion, IN: Aldersgate, 2018.

Naylor, Charles W., and Andrew L. Byers. "The Reformation Glory." *Hymnal of the Church of God.* Anderson, IN: Warner Press, 1971.

Perkins, John. *One Blood: Parting Words to the Church on Race and Love.* Chicago: Moody, 2018.

Robinson, Gene. *In the Eye of the Storm: Swept to the Center by God.* New York: Seabury, 2008.

Sanders, Cheryl. *Ministry at the Margins: The Prophetic Mission of Women, Youth & the Poor.* Downers Grove, IL: InterVarsity Press, 1997.

Smith, James Bryan. *Rich Mullins: An Arrow Pointing to Heaven: A Devotional Biography.* Nashville: B&H, 2000.

Smith, H. Shelton. *In His Image But . . . : Racism in Southern Religion, 1790–1910.* Durham, NC: Duke University Press, 1972.

Sprinkle, Preston. *People to Be Loved: Why Homosexuality Is Not Just an Issue.* Grand Rapids: Zondervan, 2015.

Strege, Merle. *I Saw the Church: The Life of the Church of God Told Theologically.* Anderson, IN: Warner Press, 2000.

Tenney, Tommy. *God's Dream Team: A Call to Unity.* Grand Rapids: Baker House, 1999.

Thurman, Howard. *Jesus and the Disinherited.* First published 1949. Boston: Beacon, 1996.

Vance, J. D. *Hillbilly Elegy: A Memoir of a Family and Culture in Crisis.* New York: HarperCollins, 2016.

Yeh, Allen. "Theology and Orthopraxis in Global Evangelicalism." In *Still Evangelical? Insiders Reconsider Political, Social, and Theological Meaning,* edited by Mark Labberton, 97–119. Downers Grove, IL: InterVarsity Press, 2018.

Index